Dr. Graff Remembers

Dr. Graff Remembers
World War II Reflections

Peter Carl Graffagnino, M.D.

Grateful Steps
Asheville, North Carolina

Publisher's note:

Written and verbal expressions considered appropriate in referring to individuals of differing gender and race and prosperity have changed in the decades since the author penned the material in this book. Rather than complying with the ever-adapting evolution of our language, we have chosen to leave undisturbed the voice of this sensitive, compassionate physician. To strictly maintain authenticity, we have not altered the author's words—those words so reflective of the times—having made only punctuation and sentence structure changes for consistency and clarity.

Grateful Steps Foundation
159 South Lexington Avenue
Asheville, North Carolina 28801

Copyright © 2014 by Robert Drury Graffagnino
Library of Congress Control Number 2014935941

Graffagnino, MD, Peter Carl
Dr. Graff Remembers
World War II Reflections

Illustration credits pages 222-224
Articles designated as previously published in
The Bulletin of the Muscogee County Medical Society
are republished with permission.

ISBN 978-1-935130-54-3 Hard Cover

Printed at Versa Press, East Peoria, IL.
FIRST EDITION

PUBLISHER'S CATALOGING-IN-PUBLICATION DATA

GRAFFAGNINO, PETER CARL.
DR. GRAFF REMEMBERS : WORLD WAR II REFLECTIONS / PETER CARL GRAFFAGNINO.
PAGES CM
ISBN: 978-1-935130-54-3 (HARDCOVER)
1. PRISONERS OF WAR—UNITED STATES—BIOGRAPHY. 2. WORLD WAR, 1939-1945—
PRISONERS AND PRISONS, GERMAN. 3. WORLD WAR, 1939-1945—PERSONAL NARRATIVES,
AMERICAN. 4. POST TRAUMATIC STRESS DISORDER—PATIENTS—UNITED STATES—
BIOGRAPHY   I. TITLE.
D805.A2 G63 2014
940.54`8173—DC23

2014935941

www.gratefulsteps.org

Dedication

The battle experience of the fighting men in World War II has been described as a journey "To Hell and Back."[1] Dr. Graff should know. He made that trip many times. His experience in the Battle of the Caves at Anzio earned him a Silver Star. His hundred-mile march at the very end of the war through the snow and ice of Northern Poland after being released from a German POW camp is no less remarkable. This grueling experience was followed by a journey into the black hole of post-traumatic stress.

Fortunately for us, Dr. Graff lived to tell his story.

This book is dedicated to the characters with whom he shared his journeys. Their names are scattered throughout these pages. Some of these individuals did not survive the war; a few remained Dr. Graff's friends and associates throughout the rest of his life. Their stories inhabited his memories, inspired his efforts as a writer and, many decades later, bring these pages to life.

This book is dedicated to them.

---

1 Audie Murphy, *To Hell and Back*, New York: H. Holt, 1949.

Table of Contents

Foreword

CAPT. PETER C. GRAFFAGNINO, M.C., U.S.A.

The Silver Star for gallantry in action at Anzio Beachhead during the period from February 15 to 23, 1944, was presented to Capt. Peter C. Graffagnino of New Orleans, La. He was in charge of an Infantry Battalion Aid Station and was the sole medical officer present at the time. The area of the Aid Station was under enemy mortar and artillery fire and was subject to enemy bombing attacks. He cared for and evacuated 104 wounded men without the loss of a life. He spent much time with front line companies, giving encouragement and medical attention to the wounded and when the battalion was ordered to a new position and it was impossible to evacuate several wounded men, he remained with the wounded and was made a prisoner of war. Dr. Graffagnino graduated from the Tulane University of Louisiana School of Medicine, New Orleans, in 1939.[2]

2From *For Courage and Devotion Beyond the Call of Duty*, citations to medical officers in the United States Armed Forces during World War II, Mead & Johnson, 1946.

Prologue

Major Peter Carl Graffagnino, M.D., my only sibling, known to me as Carl, was 11 years older than I.

Left to right: Ned, Carl and mother, Rosine Graffagnino

Before the war Carl was truly a role model for me. I followed him at a small private military day high school and at College and Medical School at Tulane University in New Orleans. He was a well liked and accomplished student, a good athlete in golf and a "bench-warming," high school footballer. Musically inclined, he played piano and banjo and was an excellent artist in pen and ink as well as water colors. His talents as an author are to be seen in these memoirs. He also had a winning personality with the coeds from Newcomb College. All of these things, needless to say, were of great interest to me as his little brother.

Here I begin my memories as experienced by our family on the homefront, beginning with his enlistment in 1941 when he was 25 years old.

After the war in Europe began in September 1939, America had begun to prepare for our possible entry into the fray. Carl at that time had begun a year of internship at Charity Hospital in New Orleans. He went on to obtain a two-year appointment as resident in Obstetrics and Gynecology at Cornell in New York. My mother, an older cousin, Lula Graffagnino, and I accompanied Carl as he drove to New York City to begin his residency in July of 1940.

Like many other American young men in 1940–41 my brother began to think about joining the armed forces and specifically as a physician. He wanted to look for enlistment as a commissioned officer. I remember his discussions with my parents about whether or not he should make this move— should he join now or finish his two years of residency? Understandably, the members of our household, which included Carl, my parents. my mother's bachelor brother, Pierino Giardina, and me, just turning 14, were concerned about what his enlistment might lead to. He received his commission in the summer of 1941 as a First Lieutenant in the U.S. Army Medical Corps, whereupon he left Cornell after completing the first of his two years of training.

We followed Carl's service from Fort Benning, Georgia, to his arrival at Fort Devens, Massachusetts, in May 1942. There he was assigned to the 45th Division. Later in 1942, while still based at Fort Devens, he met and married Jane Drury after a whirlwind, wartime courtship during which she was persuaded to break her engagement to another man. In November my parents traveled from New Orleans to Jane's home town of Leominster, Massachusetts, for the wedding.

The 45th Division's extensive training had begun in the summer of 1942, doggedly perfecting their beach landings on the shores of Cape Cod and Martha's Vineyard. From November of that year to March 1943, there was winter warfare training in Upper New York State, followed in the early spring by more practice landings on Chesapeake Bay and then on to the Blue Ridge Mountains of Virginia for mountain training.

During most of this time, we had only intermittent and fragmentary contact with him because of wartime security. The division was finally sent to the harbor at Hampton Roads, Virginia, where they boarded a convoy of some 100 troop and cargo ships on June 6, 1943, for the two-week transatlantic journey to join General George Patton's Seventh Army in North Africa.

We had to piece together his later activities indirectly from the news and from brief letters in which he told us what he was allowed to about the landings in North Africa; the invasion of Sicily under General Patton; his off-duty trip by Jeep to look up relatives in the village of Salaparuta, south of Palermo, where our father had been born; then the Salerno beachhead where the Division joined General Mark Clark's Fifth Army; the grueling winter months on the Apennine front near Cassino; and finally the Anzio beachhead where he was captured by the Germans in February 1944.

Carl later received the Silver Star for "gallantry in action at Anzio Beachhead during the period from February 15 to 23, 1944." He chose to stay behind and care for more than one hundred wounded soldiers who were not able to be moved from his front line Battalion Aid Station in the caves of pozzolana near Anzio, a position that was eventually overrun by advancing German forces. [see Silver Star citation on page ix.]

At home we all were distressed because we stopped hearing from him. Had he died? Was he injured? Was he a prisoner of war? At first we learned that he was missing in action and finally, that he was a prisoner of war in Poland at the camp known as Oflag 64.

We then began to hear directly from Carl by brief notes on post cards which were often censored with words or entire sentences blacked out. He shared with us what he could about life in the prisoner of war camp. We were very reassured to hear that he was safe and healthy. From early 1944 to early 1945 we were able to send him notes and to prepare small Red Cross packages which were forwarded to him.

After the last week of January 1945 the time of our greatest anxiety began. Once again we did not hear from him. We later learned this was because he was in the long winter march of prisoners from Oflag 64 back toward Germany as the Germans retreated in front of the advancing Russian Army.

Over the next two or three months my frantic father, Dr. Peter Graffagnino, made inquiries and finally contacted our Louisiana Congressman Jimmy Morrison. Morrison's office did a remarkable job, learning from Army contacts in postwar Europe about the progression of an American soldier-patient—who had no "dog tags" but who resembled my brother—from camps and hospitals in the Russian, British and American occupied zones in Germany to the U.S. Army Hospital in Liège, Belgium, where his identity was at last established.

Our worries multiplied when we learned he was seriously ill, suffering from malnutrition, frostbite and the most concerning, his being mentally out of contact. My parents and Jane were highly emotional. I was particularly surprised and affected when my usually taciturn Uncle Pierino, my mother's brother, who had lived with us since Carl was a child, broke down in a torrent of tears.

Our next contact came when we learned Carl would arrive by hospital ship in Charleston, South Carolina. My parents and Jane were there when the ship arrived in August of 1945, and they were devastated when they saw him physically emaciated but also non-responsive to anything and anybody in the outside world.

Carl was sent by train to the Brooke General Army Hospital in San Antonio, Texas, for treatment. Jane accompanied him there.

Meanwhile during these same months, just turning 18, I had enlisted in the Navy, and in August was in Boot Camp near Chicago.

Early in that month, President Truman had ordered the dropping of the atomic bombs on Hiroshima and Nagasaki. In September the war in the Pacific ended. On leave that month, I flew to New Orleans and, with my parents, drove to see Carl in San Antonio. Jane had been there since he had arrived.

As part of his therapy Carl had been started on a course of electroshock treatments. When we did visit with him on the ward, he was indeed somewhat, though hesitantly, responsive to us. He seemed to welcome efforts of affection from each of us. He could produce no words but only mumbled as he tried to respond to us when we talked to him. He was able to produce a few sketches for us. A good sign, we thought. My parents noted that his physical health was improving.

In the month or so that followed, Carl recovered completely. The only obvious remnant of his difficulties was his broken nose, suffered in some altercation during the march in the snow and ice from Poland to Germany. As far as we know he never later considered restorative surgery, but seemed to wear the flattened remnants of his once prominent Sicilian nose as a badge of honor for the rest of his life.

Carl and Jane went on with their lives. They returned to New Orleans in the fall of 1945, where Carl completed his residency in Obstetrics and Gynecology. There they had their two sons, Bob in 1946, and Tom in 1949. In 1950 they moved to Columbus, Georgia, where Carl established an active and successful private practice and produced the fascinating articles in *The Bulletin of the Muscogee County Medical Society* included in this book, writings that truly bring his wartime saga to life.

As a psychiatrist, I am particularly touched by Carl's engrossing description of his mental breakdown as presented in Part Four of this book. This represents a rare and most unusual insight, coming from a medically trained person, on his own observations while undergoing, as he mentions, delusions, hallucinations, manic and depressive symptoms as well as catatonia. I believe these very remarkable disclosures make an exceptional contribution to psychiatric literature.

– Paul Ned Graffagnino, M.D.

Part One

Army Training Years

An Introduction

Dr. Peter Carl Graffagnino, my father, was born in New Orleans, February 14, 1916, and died in his adopted hometown of Columbus, Georgia, on January 18, 1984, a few weeks shy of his 68th birthday.

Dad was known to his parents and to his many Sicilian immigrant family members in New Orleans during his early years by his middle name of Carl—not surprising, as his father, his grandfather and a rather significant number of uncles and cousins also bore the name of Pietro or Peter. Later in life he would not escape the even more common family nickname, becoming known to all his many friends and even to his wife as "Graff"— "Doctor Graff" to his patients and medical associates. Two of us were privileged to call him "Dad."

As will be described in these pages, June in the year of 1941 marked a significant turning point in his life. At the age of 25 he had nearly completed his medical residency at a large New York hospital, having received his undergraduate and medical school degrees at Tulane University in New Orleans. With the apparent inevitability of war in Europe and with the prospect of military service looming, he made a decision to join the Army.

The following pages contain many of his recollections of events that transpired over the next four years of his life.

Following his military service, Dad returned to civilian life and completed his medical training, eventually leaving New Orleans and resettling with his wife and two young sons in Columbus, Georgia, where he established a long and successful medical practice as a physician in the field of obstetrics and gynecology.

***

In 1962 Dad assumed his role as Editor of *The Bulletin of the Muscogee County* (Georgia) *Medical Society*, a position he would occupy for the next twenty years until his retirement. Most of the material appearing in these pages was originally published in *The Bulletin*, either as editorials, or in his monthly column titled "The Doctor's Lounge." A number of previously unpublished articles, written before he assumed his role as editor of the *The Bulletin*, were found among his papers after his death. These articles describe his early days in the Army at Fort Benning and have been inserted in their appropriate chronological sequence in this text.

Dad wrote on many subjects, and *The Bulletin* was his soap box of choice. His favorite topics seemed to be politics, the state of the medical profession, the threat of social change on the society, the country and the world. The single subject that is the focus of this book is his World War II experience as a medical officer: his training, his participation in the Allied invasion of Italy, his capture by German forces following the Battle of the Caves at Anzio and his yearlong confinement in various German Prisoner of War camps.

His wartime experiences are something he never talked much about at home; most of what I subsequently learned about them came from the incidents he described in 34 separate editorials, published sporadically over his 20 years as Editor of *The Bulletin*.

The author's material has been arranged in a chronological sequence for the reader's benefit. The original publication date of each article is documented. Because the articles were not written to appear in the order in which they are presented here, they must be appreciated as a collection of brief, and at times disjointed, flashbacks, which is how they were originally composed.

Throughout his published editorials, he exercised his prerogative as an editor to use the "editorial we" (nosism) when referring to himself.

The individual pieces are not a continuous flow of historical events but are an interesting and often insightful collection of highly personalized memories of those events, described in down-to-earth terms from the perspective of the common foot soldier caught up in the tidal wave of history. Dr. Graff succeeds in describing his experiences with an objectivity that at times belies the gravity of what was going on around him. His dispassionate style allows him to portray and to bring to life the everyday ordinariness of the experience, even though the events he describes may not seem so ordinary to us today. The boredom, the frustration and the humor of the events are woven into the fabric of the wartime experience, punctuated with poignant, and at times horrific episodes that bleed to the surface in several places, occasionally without warning.

His collection of wartime editorials ends with a description of his release at the conclusion of the war from Oflag 64, a German POW camp near what is today Sczubin, Poland, and his subsequent march in the dead of winter in early 1945 across Northern Poland with several hundred fellow prisoners. The ones who survived the brutal trek of more than 150 miles through snow and sub-zero temperatures eventually reached Szczecin near the German border, loaded onto rail cars then transported south to Luckenwalde, an Allied collection point on the outskirts of Berlin, where the surviving POWs received much needed medical attention before being sent home.

The author opens his description of his four-year ecperience with a recounting of his decision to join the Army in 1941.

– Robert Drury Graffagnino

Dr. Peter Carl Graffagnino

June 1941: Army Medicine and Col. Strong
Originally published June 1966

W ITH THE PASSAGE of a quarter of a century—always a good
point to indulge in reminiscence—we recall that at this time
of year in 1941, we were in New York City trying to make up our
mind whether to stay on in residency training or join some branch
of the armed services. (This seems to be a recurrent decision each
generation must face.) Unlike the interns and residents of today, most
of us then were single and unattached, so the added complication
of what to do about wives and families did not exist. At that time
the European war was already in progress, and it seemed obvious
that the remaining three to four years of training ahead were due
to be interrupted. In retrospect, there was no real reason to make
a hurried decision, but somehow then it did seem important to get
things settled.

Through laziness and general disinterest in all things military, we
had not had the foresight, on graduating from medical school two
years before, to sign the offered application, and as a result, did not
hold a reserve commission. Others at the hospital talked knowingly
of the advantages of the Air Corps, Navy or Army, and even of the

British and Canadian Services, but we were ignorant of all. The influence that headed us finally in the direction of Army medicine was a letter from a former close friend and classmate. He was already in service and comfortably located at the Fort Benning Station Hospital. He was looking for company. We were urged to join immediately, since the Army was still honoring requests for particular assignments. After the decision was made, we informed our chief and the hospital administrator that we would not be staying for the next year and took the subway down to 90 Church Street, where we filled out forms, had a physical examination and waited.

Two complications developed in short order. First, our eyesight, while apparently adequate for draft requirements, was below the required standards for commission as an officer. Second, to be stationed at Benning, it would be necessary to apply through the Fourth Corps Area instead of the First. Obstacles like these, however, were only minor challenges. The eyesight problem was solved by several interviews, considerable paperwork, additional examinations and by signing some sort of disability waiver form. We counted on connections in New Orleans, our native city located in the Fourth Corps Area, to deal with the second complication.

We did not fully realize how solid the connections were until mid-June when, having left New York and returned south, we stood before the proper desk in the Federal Building on St. Charles Street. Colonel Robert Strong, a friend of the family and our own former Professor of Pediatrics at Tulane, was not only the officer in charge but, by virtue of his reserve rank, also the senior medical officer in the entire Fourth Corps Area. He greeted us pleasantly and made a great show of shuffling through stacks of papers, found the right ones, made us sign one or two more forms, and assured us in an official and efficient manner that everything possible would be done to grant the commission and the assignment as requested. The papers would have to make their usual channeled movements up to Washington and back, but in due time, he was certain, all would be in order. He rose formally, and as we did not think a salute was yet in order, we merely shook his hand, expressed thanks and went our way.

One hour later, at noon, we walked into the dimly lit, air-conditioned bar in the Roosevelt and were promptly hailed by our first name from a corner alcove. The earlier visit must have terminated the morning's medical work, for there, glowing rosily in a seat against the wall, was Colonel Strong making violent motions for us to join him. His jaunty overseas cap with its silvered eagle was perched symmetrically, but transversely, across his head, running from ear to ear above the bright red of an advancing forehead. This descent from protocol was reassuring. As the conversation progressed from drink to drink, our faith in military medicine was bolstered.

Dr. Strong—it was difficult to think of him then as "the Colonel"—had always been a favorite professor. A brilliant and knowledgeable clinician, author and editor of several texts and a top authority in his field of Pediatrics, he had retained a humor and tolerance that endeared him to his students. It was rumored that he occasionally enjoyed a nip or two during working hours, and he was a familiar figure on the charity wards making rounds all alone at odd hours, handing out pennies and candies to the small patients. One of his eccentricities was that he invariably wore white tennis shoes. That day in the bar he expounded at length about the frustrations of his new job. His troubles with the Army, if indeed there were troubles, arose only from his age and rank, which unfortunately, from his viewpoint, placed him behind a desk in the corps command instead of on the road to adventure. It was a far cry from the American Expeditionary Force (A.E.F.) of WWI and the memories of what must have been a gay, gay Paree. When we left the colonel, this time with an exchange of brisk saluting, we were certain that our papers could have fallen into no better hands.

Colonel Strong never did get overseas. He commuted to his desk from the Gulf Coast (where he lived after his retirement from teaching), and, just prior to his retirement from the Army as a Brigadier General, he had become a great favorite of the M.P.s there.

Every evening after cocktail time, the general would appear at one or two of the busy intersections in Gulfport and spell the M.P.s at their posts directing traffic, while they ducked out for a quick beer. In spite of an occasional traffic snarl, his regular evening appearances were looked forward to by the military as well as the civilian residents. After his death a few years later, there was talk of erecting a memorial to him on one of the corners, but somehow it never came about. It must have gotten lost in the red tape he so despised.

Memory Lane
Originally published October 1962

THE ANNUAL JOINT meeting of the Muscogee County Medical Society and the staff of Martin Army Hospital was a successful one and well attended by both groups. We made several new acquaintances and renewed a pleasant old one with Colonel Henry W. Grady, a true officer and gentleman now retired and living in Columbus, who in other years headed the Department of Radiology at the Benning Station Hospital. Colonel Grady's presence and the date reminded us that exactly 21 years ago, with red-bordered letter in hand, we were timidly mounting the pine-shaded concrete steps of the old Post Hospital reporting for active duty "on or before 1200 hours, 10 Sept., 1941."

If our attention wandered during the very excellent and learned talk on radioisotopes, it was partly because our weakening mentality has been outdistanced by the tremendous advances in this modern field, but mostly because we were lost in a flood of memories about those earlier days of military medicine at Benning.

We remembered that, perhaps instinctively preserving our civilian status as long as possible, we did not report until just before the stipulated 1200 hours on our orders. In 1941, 10 Sept. fell on a Saturday.

As we went up the hospital steps, we were met by a horde of enlisted personnel, medical officers, civilian workers and maroon-robed patients all heading in the opposite direction. We wandered around lost for a while, and, when we finally located the proper administrative office, we were greeted by a remarkably disinterested corporal who wearily advised us without looking up from his comic book to come back on Monday when someone would be there to tell us what to do. We were gone on weekend pass before we ever really got on duty.

Ft. Benning Medical Office Building

In those pre-Pearl-Harbor months we discovered that Army medicine was considerably less strenuous than the rigors of a $10-a-month residency at a university hospital and that the duties of a Station Hospital ward officer required knowledge in fields apart from mere doctoring. Among other things, we learned about paperwork, requisitions, Section Eights, Line of Duty Boards, weekly inspections and property checks. In no time at all we became familiar with exactly how many "Pans, bed, 1 ea." we had, and along with our chief of staff, the wardmaster, we could map the weekly strategy and tactics in the constant battle over hospital property, with all the brilliance of a three-star general.

We were watching a polo game on the Sunday afternoon when the attack on Pearl Harbor was announced over the PA system. And although this did not interfere with the match in progress, it was not long before we realized that total war had come to Benning. The declaration of war by Congress set into motion all of the administrative gears and mimeographing machinery of the Post simultaneously and in grand confusion. All leaves were immediately cancelled; gas-mask and air-raid drills became daily occurrences; night blackouts were begun. Orders, countermanding orders and new orders countermanding the countermanding orders appeared at almost hourly intervals. After a couple of weeks of frenzied military efficiency, when it became evident that no dive bombers were materializing out of the blue Georgia skies and that no enemy submarines had slipped up the Chattahoochee from the Gulf to sabotage the pontoon bridge, the tension eased slightly and three-day holiday leaves were granted. Even then we were recalled from ours by an enthusiastic mimeographer, who had the countermanding orders canceling the recall ready by the time we had returned the 500 miles to the Post.

By February, in spite of the global war on two fronts, all was calm again and the hospital was back to a relaxed routine. We enjoyed an early spring on our ward among the hemorrhoids and pilonidal cysts from 8 to 4, and on the golf course after hours. We left Benning in the summer of '42 to become a foot doctor with the walking infantry, and it was another year before we finally got overseas and into combat where we could relax.

Through all the post-war years the memories of Fort Benning have always been pleasant ones—but we are glad those years are behind us (we hope).

Introduction to Ft. Benning
previously unpublished

T HERE WAS NO standardized procedure for indoctrinating new medical officers to the Army methods at that time. Although there was a course for medical personnel in operation then at the old Carlisle post in Pennsylvania, it was only required that all medical officers attend this at some time during their period of service. I somehow missed this enlightening experience, and there were moments later in my Army career when I became aware that there were obvious blank areas in my grasp of Army medical knowhow. For example, I could never remember—because, of course, I had never learned—the exact dimensions of a pit latrine, or how to set up a field "pro"-station. Fortunately, there were always able and sympathetic corpsmen who seemed to know about such things and who came to my rescue in time of stress.

Ft. Benning Main Headquarters Building.

At any rate, I headed for Fort Benning, equipped only through the advice of my classmate, an Army veteran of almost five months. In uniforms, I had concentrated mainly on summer khakis and the standard winter blouse, pinks and olive-drabs, figuring to complete my wardrobe once I was on the scene and more familiar with what might be needed. I had wisely disregarded my friend's advice to be sure and bring dress blues, but had succumbed to a tailored set of dress, summer whites, which I managed to wear once during the next five years and which, somehow, always reminded me of Nelson Eddy singing to Jeanette MacDonald.

Shortly after my arrival, too, I invested in a wide-brimmed campaign hat, with its four-dimpled peak, on the advice of our Regular Army Surgical Chief, who maintained that this was the one, stable item of wear that could be counted on to remain unchanged for years to come. Within a month a general directive had banished this relic to the museum shelves where it joined the tricorn.

Being embarrassed, and unsure of where and on what side to pin the various insignia, I decided to report for duty in civilian clothes. I can still remember the ensemble that included a Brooks Brothers gabardine suit and white and tan saddle oxfords—a combination that included my preoccupation with the competition, also in pursuit of my love, who originated out of Princeton and the University of Virginia. But the tan gabardine color did make me feel less conspicuous in a sea of khaki.

The old hospital at Benning, a starkly typical, but not unimpressive, white building of standard, hot-climate Army Hospital design, sprawled over a slight rise in a grove of tall pines. It was backed up against the second and third holes of the golf course and faced, across the road, a large area of temporary, wooden hospital buildings, connected by their endless miles of corridors.

As I moved cautiously up the tiers of concrete steps toward the main entrance, shortly before noon on Saturday, September 10, 1941, I was passed by increasing numbers of officers, enlisted men, maroon-robed patients and civilians, all heading down in the opposite direction. By the time I located the proper office inside, I was confronted by a remarkably disinterested corporal, who heard me out patiently, and then advised me to come back at eight Monday morning, when there would be somebody on duty who would know what to do with me. This blunt dismissal unnerved me, and, fighting back a desire to whimper, I set off, with the corporal's permission, to explore the main floor of the hospital, hoping to find a familiar face or some office still in operation. But it was in vain. I went so far as to peer into a couple of wards, but even these contained only one or two obviously moribund patients and a scattering of others strung up in immobilizing traction. The rest were gone on weekend pass.

Ft. Benning Station Hospital

Disheartened, but still determined, I returned and roused the corporal out of his comic book. I had him find a blank sheet of official-looking paper, and on it I stated, in as military a fashion as possible, that I had reported for duty prior to 1200 hours, as ordered, signed my name boldly and placed the message under a weight on the most important looking desk in the office. After the months of planning, I had no intention of being absent without leave, brought up for desertion or court-martialed for failure to report for duty on my first day in the Army.

Leaving the corporal, who by this time had me pegged as a new psychiatrist, to meditate on my shrewd management of the situation, I headed for off-duty.

Capt. Max Rulney
Previously unpublished

IN SEPTEMBER OF 1941 the tempo of life at the pleasant, sun-baked main post of Fort Benning, Georgia, was still moving along at the leisurely pace of a peacetime Army. The equilibrium, however, was being increasingly disturbed by the steady influx of new personnel, and the step-up in activity. The rebellious movement of the complainers, who had joined or been drafted for their "year" of service, had already passed its peak, and while the rallying cry of "O.H.I.O." (Over-the-Hill-In-October) might still crop up on occasion, it was in the half-hearted joking manner of men resigned to their fate. The broomstick guns, simulated mortars and cardboard tanks, with their background jingle of the Good Humor bells, were still part of some field maneuvers but were losing out rapidly to their counterparts. The two new jump towers for paratroop training were still objects of curiosity, and the Officer Candidate School program was just beginning to mushroom. At the Station Hospital, military medicine was still holding stubbornly to its routine of the 1930s, with only a few signs of annoyance incident to the increased patient volume and the absorption of the bewildered civilian doctors.

My first weeks of adjustment to Army medicine could hardly have been pleasanter. It was apparent from the beginning that the long-hour, seven-day-a-week, every-other-night-on-duty schedule of my previous civilian hospital years was not the way of the Army Medical Corps. We were on duty at eight and off promptly at four, and, except for a mild four-hour stint on Saturday mornings, the weekends were free. Long accustomed to the meager remuneration that was the lot of the intern and resident in the large teaching institution (a salary of 10 dollars a month my first year, that dropped to zero, my second), I could never overcome the feeling of dishonesty in accepting each month the tremendous paycheck for doing what was, by comparison, so little work.

I was classified as a surgeon—I suppose, because of my one year of added training in obstetrics and gynecology—and was assigned to a general surgical ward under the wing of Captain Max Rulney.

In the eyes of our Regular Army Chief of Surgery, the captain was a paragon in his field and the perfect combination of medical, administrative and military efficiency to which all should aspire. All new medical officers assigned to Surgery spent, by custom, an initial two-week indoctrination period under the helpful and watchful Rulney eye. Captain Rulney had served with the C.C.C.[1] until its demise, moving logically onward to the Army several years before my entry. From Max, I learned the basic tenet that there was more to Army medicine than just doctoring.

Max Rulney
Captain MC
Ward Surgeon

For one thing, there was property accountability. On taking over a ward, the new medical officer was presented with a detailed listing of all property belonging thereto, including every conceivable moveable object—from "Pans, bed 30 ea." to "Spoons, soup 60 ea." This he must sign, thereby making himself financially responsible for many thousands of dollars worth of extremely uninteresting items. (In 1941, the Medical Administrative Corps was still essentially part of the central hospital command and had not yet enlarged to absorb the lower echelon phases.) Since the weekly property check was as <u>honored a hospital</u> custom as was the colonel's Saturday morning

1 Civilian Conservation Corps.

white-glove inspection, it was imperative that all property be kept under constant surveillance.

It was doubly imperative, according to Max Rulney, to have a thoroughly seasoned non-com as Wardmaster. The qualifications for this trying job, aside from experience, included boundless energy, a glib tongue, fast clever hands, hawk eyes, swiftness of foot, the soul of a pawnbroker and friends in the right places. In any Army hospital, the right places were (and are) the mess hall, the quartermaster and the central supply. With a dullard for a Wardmaster, the innocent medical ward officer could lose half of his sheets and pillowcases on one laundry exchange, and, within a week, half of his beds could be missing. The required weekly inventory kept the constant battle over property at fever pitch, pitting ward against ward, and all against the central services, with the Wardmaster a supreme tactician mapping strategic moves and countermoves with all the brilliance of a four-star general.

The objective, of course, was not only to keep the ward's own inventory intact, but to accumulate surpluses of everything possible, in case of an enemy raid or some unforeseen disaster. Failing this, and in the event of an actual shortage, it became necessary to fall back on previous alliances, bargaining, blackmail or outright forays against the less able.

This aspect of Army medicine, while provoking and time consuming, helped to fill the otherwise dull hours of required daily duty and served, in a way, as occupational therapy for the fretful, disturbed medical officer. Even at the end of my nine months at Benning, I never became convinced the entire property tempest was not a complete illusion. It seemed logical that the property of the whole hospital was a constant amount, (actually, about half of what an accurate total inventory would show), that was juggled, swapped, stolen and stolen back at regular, weekly intervals by a grand collusion of wardmasters to meet each individual property check as it came due.

During my apprenticeship under the redoubtable Max, I learned that the strictly medical duties of the ward surgeon, aside from the time spent in the operating rooms and the occasional clinic, could be accomplished with minimum effort in about one hour of a working day. This left time for those other important duties, such as counting property, writing requisitions and reports and preparing for inspections.

Medically, however, Max did introduce me to the Army sick-call and its proper method of management. Five days a week, immediately after the lunch hour, it fell to Captain Rulney to hold sick-call in the treatment room of our ward for the enlisted men of the hospital medical detachment. Max managed this with the practiced ease of the experienced military man, who realizes that the criterion of a good officer is his ability to delegate authority. He was brisk, efficient and decisive in dealing with the few problems that filtered up to him from his subordinate staff. Once, when I was preparing to excise an ingrown toenail, in the approved fashion of my medical school and graduate training, using sterile gloves and draping the foot in sterile towels, in preparation to injecting and deadening the throbbing toe with a local anesthetic, Max stopped me with a tolerant gesture. "Lieutenant," he said, "I'm sure you will do a good job of it your way—but let me show you a simpler method."

Edging me aside, and without removing the lighted cigarette from the corner of his mouth, he spoke a few reassuring words to the apprehensive soldier, deftly inserted a hemostat under the diseased nail, clamped it shut and, with a quick twist, wrenched the entire nail from its bed. It was over in a jiffy. The astonished patient had hardly been pushed back onto the treatment table to swallow an APC capsule before the toe was dressed, and he was out of the room and on his way back to duty.

Max observed that in his long experience, the cure, using this method, was invariably a permanent one, since he had never had a patient come back with a recurrence.

Rx by the Numbers
Originally published September 1963

A FOOTNOTE IN the combat diary of the late George S. Patton tells of an incident during the World War II campaign in France when, after several weeks of continuous rain, some dry weather was desperately needed to launch an important armored offensive. The fretful Patton called for his Third Army Chaplain and commanded him to compose a prayer requesting the Almighty to dry up the heavens so that they could get on with the business of killing Germans. The Chaplain protested, but discovered in short order that it was practical to yield to the more immediate chain of command and did as he was told. The rains stopped, the advance was successful and an impressed General Patton awarded the padre a Bronze Star for coming through with a "goddamned potent prayer."

A somewhat similar incident illustrating the influence of military mind and rank on the practice of medicine occurred at the Benning Station Hospital in 1941. General Patton, then commanding the 2nd Armored in training at Benning, appeared unexpectedly in the old EENT clinic. The medical officer in charge was busy in a treatment cubicle at the time, but hearing a terrible commotion going on in the waiting area, popped out to quell the disturbance. He discovered the colorful General in the center of a furious activity that had patients, nurses, orderlies and his own entourage scurrying in all directions to bring the outside lawn benches into the clinic. Patton was a highly emotional and compassionate man, and the sight of a long line of ailing enlisted men standing and waiting their turn to be seen was too much for him. If they were sick enough to be off duty, they were sick enough to wait in more comfort. Taking in the situation at a glance, the medical officer had enough presence of mind to know that the sooner he got the General seen and treated, the easier it would be on everyone.

The General had a sore throat, and submitting impatiently to examination he remarked that his own medics had been treating him for a week without success, and he was tired of it. He made it plain that since he had taken the trouble to come in from Sand Hill, he expected to be cured, and fast. The medical officer looked at the throat, and although he felt that the laryngitis was probably due to too many cigarettes and too much bellowing on the General's part, he wisely weaseled out by telling Patton it was a common condition caused by the fumes and dust of the heavy armored vehicles. The diagnosis apparently pleased the General. Frantically groping for some new and unused, spectacular remedy, the doctor spied a nearby ultraviolet lamp and gave the General a special, if unorthodox, treatment. Patton left satisfied; in no time at all the benches were back on the lawn and peace in the clinic restored.

Two days later a captain from the 2nd Armored appeared in the clinic with high fever and badly abscessed tonsils. As the same medical officer prepared to admit him to the hospital, the captain objected. "Couldn't you give me a light treatment like the one that cured General Patton?"

"Captain, you're sick," said the doctor, "and this is an entirely different condition."

"Maybe so," said the captain, "but the General sent me over to get the lamp, and that's all the treatment he'll authorize."

The "Dirty Surgery" Ward
Previously unpublished

I SOON REALIZED, as a new medical officer in the Army, that my assignment to the Station Hospital at Benning had been a fortunate one. After the first weeks of becoming accustomed to the unfamiliar ways of Army medicine, I became aware of other medical assignments that must have required considerably greater adjustment than my own. There were the unfortunates assigned to permanent dispensary jobs, and others out with the field units on the vast Benning reservation itself, who were hardly aware that the Main Post, the Station Hospital or the Main Officers Club even existed. Occasionally one or two of these doctors would wander in for some medical get-together—bedraggled outsiders who viewed us, the chosen caste, with obvious envy and disdain. What did we know about aid stations, overnight marches, shooting azimuths or the problems of an infantry battalion?

The answer, of course, was nothing. Furthermore, we had really never even thought about such things. We were part of a different Army, and while we lived a more comfortable life, we were preoccupied with our own aggravations and annoyances. We fought the battles of paperwork, dull hours of ward duty, property counting, uninteresting clinics and the boredom of the repetitive practice of medicine on the basically healthy young men who made up the Army.

Wards 9 and 10, which I had been given, were in the permanent group of hospital buildings and were part of the "dirty surgery service." This designation came from the fact that our cases were all contaminated or infected, in contrast to "clean surgery" that dealt with non-infected problems such as hernias, appendectomies and the like. Along with boils and abscesses, we handled the hemorrhoids, rectal fistulas and pilonidal cysts. These last, the bane of Army medicine, were small vestigial, gland-like remnants located between the bony sacrum and its covering skin. Their unfortunate location made them extremely susceptible to sitting and sleeping on hard ground and to the jolting rides of Army transportation. As a result, many of these that might have remained quiescent or even unnoticed for a lifetime in a softer civilian setting were traumatized and became painfully infected. No matter what treatment was employed, from simple drainage to complicated excisions with reconstructive, plastic repair, results were distressingly poor, since the bony, sacral base did not lend itself to proper healing. Recovery took a long time, and even after an apparently satisfactory result, a return to full duty frequently caused the healed area to break down and become reinfected, making hospitalization again necessary.

I got to know many of these "pilonidal patients" quite well. A great number were on the wards when I took over, and eight months later, when I left, some of the same faces were still there. They were a cheerful group, by and large, at peace with and inured to their common infirmity. They would heal and leave, recur and return, reappearing at intervals back on the ward to a jubilant welcome with all the clamor of a class reunion at homecoming. Most of them were loyal "ward-niners" to the core, often refusing to be reassigned to other wards on the service. They were active on all of the ward projects and devoted to my scrawny, fiery, Irish nurse who ordered and herded them around like a mother hen. In the battle over property, they were invaluable defense troops, and in times of emergency, they would act as scouts, or even undercover agents infiltrating into enemy wards and returning with such useful intelligence information as the location of a hidden cache of mattress covers on D-4.

Col. Peavy
Previously unpublished

THE SURGICAL SERVICE was ruled with a firm hand and with the inflexible rules that seemed characteristically formulated by the eccentric personalities developed through long years of medical practice under the unsympathetic thumb of a peacetime military organization. Colonel Peavy, our Regular Army Chief of Surgery, insisted that we be on our wards at eight in the morning, and remain there, always available, until the four o'clock off-duty siren sounded. We were excused only for our required presence in the operating rooms, clinics and conferences, or impromptu appearances at gas-mask or air-raid drills.

It made no difference that our work could be accomplished within two hours, our presence for the remaining six was still mandatory. By virtue of unscheduled appearances at odd hours of the morning or afternoon, the colonel kept us in a state of constant apprehension—and at our desks. Since all reading material, even medical journals, was taboo during working hours, we kept such things hidden in the back of desk drawers, reading surreptitiously, but always with an open and handy chart on the desktop and an ambulatory patient on sentry duty to sound the alarm at the colonel's approach.

Another eccentricity of Colonel Peavy was his belief that a surgical service could be effectively run only by medical officers who were unmarried. His logical military mind reasoned that single officers, by necessity, must live in the hospital quarters, thereby being available at any hour, day or night. Married officers, on the other hand, usually lived away from the hospital, even off the post many miles away. (If the married officer's family was not with him, it made no difference to the colonel, since it might appear at Benning at any moment.) In addition, he felt that the married officer's preoccupation with other problems such as wife, young children, household worries and a thousand other distractions, diluted his interest, not only in medicine, but in Colonel Peavy's surgical service in particular. As a result, and a somewhat paradoxical one, whenever a request came for a medical officer to be sent to some grim post or to an overseas assignment, it was invariably the poor doctor with the wife and four children and a newly purchased house, who was chosen by the colonel. The attached, restless bachelors remained.

Three of us, all first lieutenants and single, had neighboring rooms in the hospital barracks quarters: Bill Love, a general surgeon, Lee Blackman, a dentist, and myself. We moved more or less in the same orbit, shared similar interests and spent most of our off-duty daylight hours on the golf course that was conveniently available just behind the hospital. Our bachelor group was usually joined by one or the other of our former barracks cronies, Bell Harvard, (a urologist and my original friend and medical school classmate), and Ken Sharretts, another general surgeon. They were first lieutenants, like us, but married and now living off the post in a newly developed housing area.

Nearly every day, promptly at four, we were on our way to the first tee. Some caution had to be employed, however, because Colonel Peavy, our Chief, was also an avid golfer. The time from the first blast of the off-duty siren to the appearance of the colonel on the first tee represented the shortest possible interval in which this movement from hospital to golf course could be accomplished. If we were a hole or two ahead of the colonel, he knew automatically that we must have slipped away from our wards ahead of time. Consequently, before starting out ourselves,

Wm. G Love, Jr.
First Lieutenant, M.C.
Surgical Service

we learned to be careful and would lurk behind bushes or the corner of the clubhouse until we were sure the colonel had teed off.

First Lts. Harvard, Sharretts, Blackman and Love

Previously unpublished

SINCE EVENINGS AROUND the bachelor quarters in the wooden barracks were uniformly dull, the three of us who were single would descend as one, almost nightly, on the home of either the Harvards or the Sharretts for a taste of family life and fellowship over highballs. If we were at the Sharretts, the Harvards would join us, and vice versa. We spent the time getting pleasantly stoned and listening to the Sharretts' collection of records. There may have been more, but I am sure that we never got beyond the three favorites of the Sharretts, which were kept on top of the pile. One was a collection of South African Veldt folk songs, another was a wailing rendition of "I'm Thinking Tonight of My Blue Eyes" and the last was a recording of Stanley Holloway, the Lancashire Lad, singing Anne Boleyn ("with 'er 'ead tooked underneath 'er arm"). I mention these only because we played them nightly and because to this day I can recall every note and lyric of all three.

Bell M. Harvard
First Lieutenant, M.C.
Ward Surgeon

Our bachelor threesome automatically assumed that we were invited for supper, which we stayed for every evening. This was especially hard on the Harvards who had just gotten married. Anne Harvard, married on a three-day pass, was lifted bodily from the social whirl and a recently completed debutante season in New Orleans to the full duties of honeymooning and housekeeping in a two-bedroom, brick cottage surrounded by pine trees, red clay and lonely men. She could hardly have anticipated cooking for five or seven, nightly, from the fourth day of her married life onward.

But like so many of the helpless flowers of the Old South, her soft-spoken veneer covered a core of steel, and she managed us all admirably. In fact, looking back over those pleasant days of our five-sided honeymoon, I seem to recall that the whisky, food, cooking and dish-washing around the newly established Harvard household was supplied in great part by the non-sleeping-in bachelors. Annie was nobody's fool.

Fall of 1941: A Thanksgiving Dinner
Previously unpublished

T HE PLEASANT FALL passed quickly. At Thanksgiving time, Blackman and I worked for two days gathering supplies and stuffing our first turkey; Love, a graceful master at avoiding the distasteful, spent his time testing the Scotch. But we turned out a dinner for ten, which, by the time we ate it, was obscured in alcoholic fog. My true love, who had driven with her sister to spend Thanksgiving with us, left abruptly for home the next morning. Not too long afterward, she just as abruptly married an Air Corps Lieutenant from a fighter group conveniently stationed in New Orleans. I have never really yet found out whether it was my cooking that turned the tide against me.

A very short time after that, on a Sunday afternoon in early December, we were all watching a polo game on the field opposite the golf course when the announcement came, between chukkers that the Japanese had just bombed Pearl Harbor. Though the game continued, we were a thoughtful group that night. The war, it seemed, was really on.

The declaration of war by the Congress set into motion all of the administrative gears and mimeographing machinery of the Post simultaneously and in grand confusion. All leaves were immediately cancelled; gas masks and air-raid drills became daily occurrences; practice blackouts at night were begun. Orders, countermanding orders and new orders countermanding these appeared at almost hourly intervals. Finally, after about two weeks—when it appeared evident that no dive-bombers

Lee F. Blackman, Jr.
First Lieutenant, D.C.
Operative Section Dental
Clinic, Dispensary A

were materializing out of the blue, Georgia skies and no submarines had slipped up the Chattahoochee River from the Gulf to sabotage the pontoon bridge across the river to Alabama—the tension eased slightly and three-day holiday leaves were granted.

Because of my deteriorating affair of heart, I took off in the direction opposite to New Orleans to spend my leave with friends in Tryon, North Carolina. I arrived on New Year's Eve, after a cold and rainy six-hour drive, to find a telegram waiting, which stated that all leaves had again been cancelled and ordered an immediate return to duty. Still respectful of authority, I obediently returned to Benning and arrived back after an all-night drive, only to find that a second telegram had been sent, rescinding the previous one. But I was too tired to do anything but go to sleep.

January 1942: Reply by Endorsement
Originally published January 1972

RECENTLY A PATIENT presented me with a copy of her husband's orders. It was to confirm his transfer of assignment from Fort Benning and establish her eligibility for CHAMPUS (Civilian Health Medical Program Uniformed Services). Listed at the bottom left under the heading, "Distribution:" were 17 different departments, headquarters and individuals for which copies totaling 138 in number were to be supplied.

Government bureaucracy, and especially armed service bureaucracy, has long had a love affair with paperwork in order to cover every possible contingency, plug every loophole and diffuse responsibility. Contemplating the inordinate amount of secretarial work, time and paper consumed in providing just this one individual transfer order recalled an initial shattering experience with the paperwork of a Line of Duty Board in the Army thirty years ago.

In January 1942, after four months in the Army assigned to the old Station Hospital at Benning, I was just becoming adjusted to the duties of a 1st Lieutenant in the Medical Corps. Out of the blue one day came notification (in triplicate) of my assignment as medical officer on a three-man Line of Duty Board. By mistake, since my date of rank was the most recent of the three, I was listed as the Presiding Officer. The other two members, 1st Lieutenant Evans (Infantry) and 2nd Lieutenant Hellman (Signal Corps), turned out to be novices, also.

In panic, I sought out a knowledgeable army surgeon, Captain Max Rulney (three years of doctoring in the C.C.C. and three years in the Army), whose expertise in paperwork far exceeded that in medicine. The obvious irregularity in assigning me as presiding officer upset Max greatly, but, as a practical man well versed in the devious ways of the military, he recommended not attempting to straighten out the mistake about date of rank. The paperwork, he said, might become so involved that it would be easier for the board to meet as constituted, turn in its report and have done with it.

Peter C. Graffagnino
First Lieutenant, M.C.
Surgical Service

Besides, as the senior presiding officer, I would be merely a figurehead and the actual work would fall to the lowly 2nd Lieutenant Hellman who, automatically, was the recording secretary.

The large-scale Louisiana maneuvers had ended in the fall, and, as part of the exercise, the evacuation channels for casualties were being tested. The Station Hospital at Benning had been designated as a base hospital outside of the combat zone to which wounded were shipped for definitive treatment and rehabilitation. When recovered, the evacuee would either be returned to his original unit, reassigned elsewhere, reclassified or retired as the case demanded. The particular job of our Line of Duty Board was to investigate the broken leg injury of a maneuver casualty and establish a Yes or No answer to the simple question of whether the injury had occurred "in line of duty."

Before convening the board for its first meeting, I thought it wise to visit the orthopedic wards across the road in the cantonment area to find and interview our casualty. Landry, Jules A. Pfc. was a pleasant, non-complaining draftee with his left leg encased in a walking cast. His name and unmistakable Cajun accent indicated he was a Louisiana lowland native. He was cooperative and happy to talk with a fellow Louisianan and gave a detailed straightforward account of his earlier accident.

Landry had moved with his infantry unit from Camp Blanding in Florida to Louisiana for the maneuvers. Early one Sunday morning, after a strenuous week of simulated combat, his company was out of action and in reserve, bivouacked in a spot less than a mile from his home. The thought of Sunday dinner and some of Mama Landry's crawfish bisque was too much for Jules. So, with nothing to do and being afraid to awaken his sleeping platoon sergeant to ask for permission, he took off down the familiar road and spent the day with his admiring family. After lunch, he took Alcide, a 4-year-old younger brother, for a ride on the family mule. Returning home, the mule balked, Jules was thrown and snapped both bones in his lower leg. The family took him to old Dr. St. Amant in the nearby town who splinted the leg, loaded Jules in a car and delivered him back to his company area. Unfortunately, by this time, Landry had been listed as AWOL on the daybook and the report had gone too far through channels to be retrieved.

This, essentially, was the bare story of Landry, Jules A., Pfc. and his broken leg. Our board held a meeting and decided, in view of the locale of the accident and Landry's being officially AWOL, that the injury obviously had not occurred "in line of duty." Lieutenant Hellman prepared the report consisting of our decision along with 20 pages of statements, X-ray findings and true copies of medical and other reports (all in quintuplicate). With much relief we all signed and sent it off through channels.

Two weeks later the report was back on my desk with an added front sheet marked "Urgent" and something called a "1st Wrapper Endorsement." It had apparently gotten no farther than the Station Hospital's own administration office and had been returned for "revision and correction."

Again seeking help, I approached the redoubtable Captain Rulney, who was sympathetic but not at all surprised. Max pointed out some glaring errors in phraseology, the absence of certification on a number of true copies and, worst of all, that the inexperienced Hellman had typed using half-inch margins instead of the required one-and-a-half. From his files, he supplied a standardized Line of Duty proceedings report to be used as an example, and certainly by comparison, ours was definitely the work of amateurs.

Armed with the original report and the example, I went across post to the Signal Corps area, only to find that 2nd Lieutenant Hellman had been transferred to Alaska two days before. Lieutenant Evans was easier to find, but, unfortunately, he was leaving immediately on a 10-day field exercise. He did promise to take over as recording secretary as soon as he got back.

Discouraged (and worried about that "Urgent," 1st Wrapper Endorsement), I prepared the second report myself paying careful attention to word sequence, terminology and margins. Evans signed when he got back, and the new, revised report (in quintuplicate) along with the original report and its Wrapper Endorsement was sent on its way again. This time it got as far as the Main Post Headquarters. When it reappeared on my desk three weeks later, there was another "Urgent" and a 3rd Wrapper Endorsement (what had happened to the 2nd Wrapper was never explained). It was sent back for "completion" this time and apparently needed a statement (and five true copies) from the civilian physician who had originally treated Pfc. Landry. This required some doing since old Dr. St. Amant was not a letter writer by nature, nor had he yet been paid for his efforts. When finally his grudging reply did come, copies were made and certified, and a complete new third version of the board proceedings was retyped. In the interval, however,

Lieutenant Evans had been transferred to a port of embarkation and was not available for signing. So true copies of his orders had to be obtained along with a certified statement from his former commanding officer and sent along with the report. While Evans' departure simplified matters in regard to calling board meetings, it left me wary, and, as the new report along with the previous two went off, I had no doubt that I would be seeing them all again before long.

They got to Corps Headquarters this time, and it was five weeks before they reappeared. Marked "Urgent" again and sporting innumerable new Wrapper Endorsements, another signed statement from Pfc. Landry was needed now. A quick trip to the Orthopedic wards confirmed the certainty that Landry, Jules A., Pfc. had long since departed and been returned to his unit in Florida. From other sources, it was learned that Landry's division was already in transport overseas. Nothing was left at Fort Benning but a harried Presiding Officer and the growing stacks of papers and Wrapper Endorsements. There was nothing to do except to add a statement from the orthopedic ward officer and a summarizing acid appraisal of my own, and, all in quintuplicate, the new report and the three old ones were packaged up and sent off again.

Before the calculated time for its next reappearance—it must have reached Washington on this trip, since it was gone more than five weeks—orders came through transferring me to the 45th Division at Fort Devens, Massachusetts.

The final outcome of Pfc. Landry's Line of Duty Board remains in limbo. I was haunted during the entire time of combat in Italy by a fear that the next runner coming up the rocky path to the aid station in the mountains above Cassino would be carrying a manila-wrapped package bulging with those familiar papers, requesting that I reply by endorsement. And even now, 30 years later, there is a feeling of unease on seeing any suitably sized, official-looking package that measures more than two feet in depth.

Col. William H. Schaefer, U. S. Army, Ret.
Originally published December 1963

L AST MONTH WE attended a pleasant gathering at White's Bookstore where retired Colonel William H. Schaefer was autographing his newly published book on economics, *Shares*. It is a small and interesting volume written in parable form. It explains in painstakingly simple and logical fashion the monetary system and its fallacies, and at the end it offers some of Colonel Schaefer's uncluttered thinking on what should be done about this mess.

We have been an admirer of the colonel for many years. His unfortunate capture early in the Mediterranean campaign of World War II and his subsequent long incarceration as a German prisoner of war interrupted an outstanding military career and deprived the Army and the country of a personality who would have been one of its top general officers. Colonel Schaefer might best be described in the words of Dr. William Bean, who spoke of an eighteenth-century English physician as a man who ". . . has lived a life of quiet rebellion against some of the organized asininities of contemporary existence." From our own past experience, we can vouch for Colonel Willie's rebelliousness, his integrity and intellect and his direct, forceful approach to problems.

In the summer of 1942, as a Battalion Surgeon with Colonel Schaefer's 500-man special force, we accompanied this first unit to undergo training at the newly established Army Commando Training Center on the south shore of Cape Cod.

The installation was so new that we spent the first week clearing brush, digging latrines, building facilities and making the area habitable. Along with a rigorous training program, we were supposed to be learning the amphibious techniques of shore-to-shore landings.

As so often happens in military planning, the initial confusion was great. Landing craft were scarce in those days, and the one or two dozen needed to float our embryonic commandos had to be obtained from four different commands—the Coast Guard, the Navy, the Marines and the Army Engineers. There was inter-service rivalry, and each command seemed reluctant to part with any of its hoarded craft. Coordination of the boat activities was a continuous nightmare. Then an unexpected medical catastrophe occurred when 300 of our men turned up one day at sick-call with the typical rash of a contact dermatitis. Emergency gallons of calamine lotion were rushed to us from the hospital at nearby Camp Edwards, but for three days all training was disrupted. We soon discovered that the hand to hand combat course had been laid out in a pure stand of poison ivy. Adding to the confusion and to the frustration of Colonel Schaefer and his itchy, pink-colored commandos was the fact that the permanent training command staffs in charge of the center were not only inexperienced in basic knowledge of infantry tactics, but also unbelievably bumbling and incompetent.

At the halfway mark Colonel Schaefer could stand it no longer. He called a special meeting of all officers, his own and all of the training command group. In his deliberate fashion he enumerated each day-by-day mistake, each inefficiency, each foul-up and each indignity that he and his men had had to put up with. At the conclusion of his controlled tirade, he announced with unmistakable authority (he was West Point, and outranked the commander of the school) that henceforth he was taking over and would be in charge of all activities.

The last half of our training went off like clockwork. On completing our course we had become adequately amphibious, and as a final exercise had subdued the island of Martha's Vineyard in a joint assault with the paratroopers. On graduation we were reviewed by Secretary of War Stinson and a cadre of Pentagon high brass, who were on hand to observe and officially dedicate the new school. They were most impressed.

Army training exercise, Martha's Vineyard, Summer 1942

Many years later Colonel Schaefer told us that the Secretary of War had indeed been so impressed, that on his return to Washington, he ordered an immediate blanket promotion of one grade for every man of the permanent training school command.

Even now, 21 years later, Colonel Schaefer still gets mad when he thinks about it.

Major James and the Day We Captured Martha's Vineyard (and the Joys of Field Medicine)
Originally published October 1978

THE NEWS LAST month that philanthropist Jackie Onassis had bought some 375 acres of Martha's Vineyard to help preserve the environment reminded us that it was just this time of year, 36 years ago, when we landed on that island and captured the airport at Oak Bluffs.

At the time, we were part of a special commando force and our leader on that foray was Major Chet James.

James, a small-town politician in his forties, was one of those civilian soldiers who had come up through the Colorado National Guard. In spite of his more than two years' experience on active duty, the major was about as unimpressive a specimen of "officer and gentleman" as could be imagined. Throughout the Regiment he was known as "Joe Blow," a large, bombastic, florid man with dissipated eyes, loose jowls and a prominent, sagging paunch, who pursued, with consuming interest, wine, women and song. He was not one of our favorites.

Major Chet James

Earlier, in mid-summer and as part of a five-hundred-man special unit from the Division, we had helped to inaugurate the nation's first commando training school on the south shore of Cape Cod near Falmouth, where we had learned about landing craft and shore-to-shore invasion tactics. In the early fall of 1942, as a last-full-scale maneuver before packing up to join General Patton on the North African invasion, the entire regiment moved to Cape Cod for training; its final exercise was to invade and capture Martha's Vineyard.

Because of our previous commando training, part of our medical section and part of Company I (about 150 of us in all) split away from the regimental bivouac and returned to the commando school area a few miles away. We were assigned the special task, in a joint mission with a unit from the 82nd Airborne, of capturing the island airport. While the main force of the Regiment was invading the south end of the island, we were to land, and the paratroopers were to drop, some 22 miles away on the northeast corner near Oak Bluffs.

The fall weather was beautiful, and the pre-invasion plans and training proceeded on schedule. On the day before the island-taking exercise, we even had the added treat of flying over the island with some of the airborne officers in one of their DC-3s on a reconnaissance mission to spot the landing beaches.

Some hours after midnight our small commando group (with properly blackened faces) began loading into the 12 small landing craft that were to ferry us across the seven-mile channel to Martha's Vineyard. We rode in the command boat with our intrepid leader, Major James, and Major Woodcock, the handsome, authentic British commando veteran of the Dieppe and Tobruk raids who was advisor to the new training school. We followed immediately behind the navigating Navy patrol boat, with the rest of the landing craft strung out in file behind us. At this early stage of amphibiousness, there was no radio communication between boats, and the main concern during the dark channel crossing was to keep the small, green stern light of the craft ahead in view at all times.

For the first half of the journey no problems arose. The two majors, who had been at a Cape Cod night spot, partying and drinking almost up to the moment of departure, slumped comfortably in the stern of our boat and, in a matter of minutes, lulled by the steady throb of diesel motors, were sound asleep. As the only other officer aboard, we felt obliged to stay awake, particularly since we had a young and inexperienced Navy coxswain at the helm who tended to get drowsy, allowing the green light ahead almost to disappear in the foggy blackness. We just had to hope that there were other conscientious light watchers in the 11 boats strung out behind us. By a combination of constant chatter and frequent prodding, we kept the coxswain alert and at his task for the entire journey.

We were supposed to land at dawn and, sure enough, just as the darkness began to fade, there were the bluffs and the correct beach immediately in front of us. The Navy patrol swung away and our group of LCPS, still about a half-mile from shore, went into a circling rendezvous formation in preparation for the dash toward shore all abreast.

As the light improved it became evident that only eight boats were circling, but in view of our previous amphibious experiences (and, in fact, all subsequent ones) we considered the accomplishment remarkable—the right beach, the right time and two-thirds of the boats still afloat. We later learned that two of the boats were picked up 40 miles out at sea by the Coast Guard, another landed on the northern tip of Cape Cod 50 miles away, and the other made a perfect dawn landing on the same beach we had left only a few hours before.

Just as we approached the beach, the planes came over and the pale, pink and orange dawn sky began to fill with the multicolored chutes of the paratroopers. In our command boat the two majors slept soundly on until jolted awake by the keel grinding to a sudden stop on an offshore sandbar.

James lurched to his feet unsteadily, took in the surroundings and, pleased with what he saw, bellowed, "By God, Woodcock! Right on target!" then, grandly assuming command, roared, "Over the sides, men! Get to that airport before the paratroopers land." We went over the sides into waist deep water and waded to shore with the surf breaking on our backs.

By 9:00 a.m. our special mission was over. The Infantry had landed; the paratroopers had landed; the airport had been properly captured. There was only one casualty—a paratrooper with a fractured tibia, and we had him splinted and comfortable. We ate a K-ration breakfast on the airport turf and sprawled in the warm sun to dry out our soaked shoes and woolen clothes.

At 10:00 the planes arrived; the paratroopers packed their gear, waved goodbye, loaded into the transports and flew back to Fort Bragg. Our boats, however, had returned to the Cape after landing us; they were needed to shuttle the last units of the Regiment over to the beaches on the south end. We stayed at the airport, enjoying the rest and, at one o'clock, ate a K-ration lunch.

A short time later it dawned on James that there was no way for us to get back to the mainland except with the rest of the Regiment. After fussing and fuming a while longer, he also discovered that there was no motor transportation on the island available to pick us up.

There was nothing to do but set out on foot for the other end of the island, 22 miles away.

It was a long and miserable march along deserted roads. The summer colony inhabitants had long since left the island and most of the roadside stands and stores were closed for the season. We were already tired from lack of sleep, and our salt-encrusted clothes and shoes added to the walking misery. When we stopped for a chow break at 5:30 in the afternoon, we still had more than eight miles to go. We collapsed on the roadside, but before we could relax to tackle still another delicious K-ration meal, a runner from the head of the column appeared. "Doc," said the messenger, "the major wants you up ahead. He says it's an emergency."

We struggled erect slowly, shouldered our pack and medical kit and limped painfully on our bruised and blistered feet past the long line of resting GIs to the head of the column. Major Woodcock was snoozing. James was sitting against a rock resting. He was eating a real sandwich and drinking a cold beer; one shoe was off, and a beefy foot was propped up on his Musette bag.

"I got me a blister, Doc. Fix it up for me," Joe Blow said—and he went on eating and drinking.

Chet James died of cirrhosis many years ago, back in his small town in the Colorado Rockies where he operated and owned a gas station. It took us a long time to forget that painful march and the capture of Martha's Vineyard. Reluctantly at first, but openly later, we grew to admire old Joe. He was one of those paradoxes of a wartime Army—a sorry, degenerate boozer as a stateside soldier, a magnificent, clear-headed combat leader overseas when real bullets were flying and the chips were down. It takes all kinds to run an Army.

Part Two

The Italian Campaign

June 1943: Off to War

Originally published June 1968

Twenty-five years ago, standing there on the open dockside under a noonday, coastal Virginia sun that steamed the humid 96-degree atmosphere, our thoughts about War, Army medicine and life in the Infantry were all unprintable. There was no shelter from the brightness, and the sweat soaked through clothing under the full combat pack and dripped from our wrists. A scattering of wilted Red Cross ladies offering paper cups of lemonade and melting ice did their best to spread cheer against insurmountable odds. We had been up before dawn, and, staggering under the load of full equipment, a Valpak and two barracks bags, we had hurried and waited over and over again on the move that took us from the swampy staging area of Camp Patrick Henry to the embarkation docks at Hampton Roads. The large, gray Navy transport that loomed above us at the dock was the familiar *U.S.S. Thomas Jefferson* on which we had trained in ship-to-shore amphibious techniques just two months before on a then icy Chesapeake Bay.

The 45th Division, after almost three years of training, was about to set sail finally for an overseas destination and long-awaited combat.

(The 45th, along with its sister unit from the Southwest, the 36th Division, were the first two National Guard Divisions activated by President Roosevelt on August 1, 1940 ". . . to serve in the military service of the United States for a period of 12 consecutive months, unless sooner relieved.")

We had joined the Division over one year before at Fort Devens, Massachusetts, on the same set of orders that included George Schuessler of Columbus, Lee Powers of Savannah and Bon Durham of Americus. The 45th, with two regiments from Oklahoma and one from Colorado, was already a veteran and seasoned outfit when it was sent from Texas to New England and was preparing for an immediate overseas move when we were assigned to it in May 1942. But those plans fell through, as did the next ones in September 1942 (when General Patton arrived on the scene to deliver an impassioned pep talk that included us in the task force to invade North Africa), and instead the Division had continued to train, unendingly, it seemed to most of the men. In the summer there had been two prolonged amphibious training exercises in shore-to-shore work on Cape Cod and Martha's Vineyard; from November to March the Division had endured winter maneuvers in the bitter cold and snows of upper New York State close by the Thousand Islands; and during spring, more amphibious training with the Navy on Chesapeake Bay, and then a month of mountain training in the wilderness of Virginia's Blue Ridge chain.

It had been a strenuous but healthy, pleasant and unpleasant year. Our assignment as a Battalion Surgeon with the 157th (Colorado) Regiment had been quite a change from the dull routine of hospital duty during the previous year at Fort Benning. In medical circles, such an assignment to field duty with an infantry battalion was generally considered on a par with banishment to Outer Siberia. Field units had difficulty keeping such jobs filled since immediately on assignment there was a panicky scramble on the part of any rational medical officer to get the hell out by any means available— whether it be by writing a congressman, aggravating a silent ulcer, feigning insanity or admitting to homosexuality. Consequently, it was only when an outfit was on the verge of overseas shipment that these positions could be filled with unfortunates who, lifted from this post or that on sudden order, were given no time to escape. Of the six of us who were sent to the 157th new medical officers in May 1942, only two still remained a year later. But again the positions had been filled in the staging area, and this time, for the four new doctors, there was no way out.

Dr. P.C. Graffagnino

It had been a year of medical stagnation—screening healthy young men, giving shots, holding the endless successions of sick-calls—a year of headaches, sore feet, aching backs, coughs, colds, sore throats and loose bowels. "Riding the sick book" was an easy way to avoid strenuous duty or an unpleasant garbage detail. And we could always count on a full house in the aid station on days when a 20-mile training march was scheduled. We learned to deal with the psychosomatic ailments of the chronic complainers and goof-offs. (The sick-call technique of "Iodine Jake" Holnitsky, the nutty medical officer from the 3rd Battalion who sported a Groucho Marx moustache and read Plato from a paperback, was to paint everything from a sore throat to a sore rectum liberally with gentian violet.) The only elective surgery consisted of wart and mole removals; an ingrown toe nail was a major case. The infrequent circumcision took on the aspect of a stomach resection, and we would draw straws for the privilege of being an "operating surgeon" again. We inspected barracks, latrines, shower room duckboards, mess halls, pots, pans and garbage cans. A Boy Scout with a merit badge in first aid could have performed most of our medical duties.

But there had been compensations. There was pleasure in discovering the real function of the Army and participating in the activities of infantry training and tactics. Life was seldom dull. The new world of the foot soldier, with its incessant grousing, elemental English and Rabelaisian humor was always interesting. We were fortunate in having "Uncle Charlie" Ankcorn as our Regimental Commander, a stern father-figure whose erect and dignified military bearing combined firm discipline with great ability, calm wisdom, understanding and a quiet sense of humor.

The 157th, under his guidance as National Guard Advisor to the State of Colorado in the prewar years and under his command since its activation as a unit, had matured into a capable regiment that functioned smoothly with a minimum of confusion and flap. Colonel Ankcorn was never flustered by the inconsistencies of conflicting regulations or directives that emanated from Division or higher headquarters; he merely sidestepped or ignored them. He had the respect of everyone, and the men were devoted to him and the Regiment. In that year we had discovered the meaning of esprit de corps.

The year had passed quickly. There were memories of long training marches and overnight field problems along the picturesque back roads and byways through the woodlands and orchards of the beautiful, summer and fall New England countryside. On the longer marches, after the first hours when the joking and chatter would subside, there was little joy in marching for marching's sake alone, and the steady clomp of heavy GI shoes in monotonous cadence had a sedative, hypnotic effect on all the senses. There were pleasant recollections of weekend leaves spent in Boston, New York, Baltimore, Vermont and New Hampshire. Of long walks along the isolated beaches of Cape Cod during the weeks of Commando and amphibious training. Of the coordinated, dawn landing at Oak Bluffs on Martha's Vineyard, wading through the heavy surf and watching the hazy, pink sky fill with the multicolored chutes of paratroopers and their equipment arriving to join us.

Colonel "Uncle Charlie" Ankcorn

There was pleasure in recalling the vast expanses of clean, white snow and drifts that blanketed Pine Camp and upper New York State through the winter months, the crystalloid trees and the two-story long icicles that hung from the eaves of the barracks, the poker games in the quarters that lasted for days on end during the blizzard times when the temperature hung at a steady 30 below and training had to be suspended. There were memories of a wintry Chesapeake Bay and scrambling down the ice-coated, chain-link nets over the sides of the transport ships into the bobbing landing craft below, drenched by freezing spray. Of the wild, night rides by Jeep, with Father Barry, the Regimental Chaplain, dodging trees up the rocky streambeds of the Pope and other, unnamed, peaks in the Blue Ridge. And the vivid picture, as the mountain maneuvers ended, of a group of us squatting around a borrowed, field kitchen burner unit on a sloping, desolate clearing at three in the morning drenched by a steady drizzle, brewing K-ration coffee in our canteen cups. Too miserable to move, too wet to care, too tired to complain, we could only stare, as if in a trance, at the flickering blue flames and wonder if the night would ever end, or if we should ever be warm and dry again.

But all that was behind us, and the last two weeks of confinement—in the mosquito-infested area at Patrick Henry, cut off from family and the outside world and aggravated by the endless examinations and equipment checks of the staging process—had played havoc with morale. The men were irritable, exhausted and overtrained; they were anxious to get moving, anywhere. The long waits were frustrating, and the unbearable, smothering heat on the embarkation dock was the final indignity.

Moving at a snail's pace, we filed up the gangway and were checked aboard. It was better there, but not much. The officers on the upper decks were crowded, eight to a small stateroom; the men were crammed like sardines below decks and into the holds that were already filled with supplies, weapons, vehicles and equipment. When the ship pulled away from the dock, it was only to move a short way out into the harbor where it dropped anchor. We remained there for four more days. Each morning and each night we practiced the familiar boat drills—over the sides and down the cargo nets with full equipment, into the waiting landing craft, around to the other side of the ship where we scrambled up other nets back on board again.

We felt like caged monkeys. Then on the morning of June 6, 1943, we awakened to the throb of engines and blasts of whistles. We moved slowly out of the harbor, and the giant armada of more than 100 ships that carried the 45th Division and all of its attached supporting units, headed out into the Atlantic.

July 1943: Camerina, Sicily
Originally published July 1968

O N THE AFTERNOON of June 21, 1943, the convoy that carried the 45th Division overseas passed quietly through the Strait of Gibraltar. We lined the rails of our transport, the *U.S.S. Thomas Jefferson,* to view the big rock and wondered jokingly what had happened to the Prudential Insurance sign. It was our first sight of land since leaving the Virginia coast 13 days before. The trip across had been a smooth and uneventful one. On only two occasions had there been submarine alerts, and the destroyer escorts had sped by dutifully to drop their depth charges; if any actual danger existed, it had never materialized. Although the amateur astronomers and navigators aboard had predicted a course toward North Africa, it was not until we saw Gibraltar that we knew for certain our destination lay in the Mediterranean.

Our 2nd Battalion of the 157th Infantry along with its attached supporting units constituted a complete combat team that occupied the entire transport. We were tightly packed aboard, literally in layers, with all of our ammunition, supplies, weapons and vehicles, ready to be unloaded over the sides into the landing craft that would assault an enemy beach. The repetitive training had continued throughout the voyage over. By day there were lectures, training films and calisthenics; at night, under blackout, we practiced the boat team assembly drills. Medical duties on board were minimal, and most of the time apart from the scheduled training was spent in our bunks or in the wardrooms playing gin rummy. The ordered, clean Navy life in "officer country" was an unfamiliar experience to us of the earthy Infantry, and the Navy mess with its white tablecloths, gleaming silver and colored mess-boys, was a world that recalled a pleasant life of pre-Army days.

Morale, which had reached its lowest point prior to sailing, had returned with the anticipation of imminent combat. But it slumped anew when, after being confined to the transports for four days in the harbor at Oran, we moved eastward only a few miles along the coast to Mostaganem to make still another practice landing. Once more it was down the landing nets into the landing craft and onto the beaches. The "enemy" opposing us was our old buddies from Cape Cod, troops of the 36th Division. On hand also to greet us as we stumbled dispiritedly across the sand was the flamboyant General Patton. Resplendent in polished helmet, gleaming cavalry boots and ivory-handled pistols, he strode up and down the water's edge, urging us to "Charge!" with flicks of his riding crop. We were hardly inspired.

The morale was even lower by the end of 11 days on land and more training. The dry, alkaline barrenness of French North Africa was unpleasantly hot; water was at a premium; flies, mosquitoes and fleas surrounded us; and small, grisly scorpions invaded our clothes, shoes and bedding. At higher headquarters final plans and preparations were being made for "Operation Husky," but it was not until we had loaded back on the transports and the convoy was underway again that we learned we were to invade that ancient island battleground, Sicily.

The three-cornered island, located strategically in the Mediterranean off the toe of Italy, had endured invasions and occupations with monotonous regularity for more than three thousand years. The Sicils and Sicilians, original inhabitants (and probably foreigners themselves) from the Stone and Bronze Ages, were first invaded in recorded history by the Phoenicians prior to 1500 B.C. Then in succession came the Carthaginians, Greeks,

Romans, Vandals, Ostrogoths and the Byzantine Turks. In the eighth century A.D. the Arabs took over for 300 years until displaced by the Normans, who, in turn, lost out to Spain and the House of Aragon in 1300. The Bourbon Dynasty and the Kingdom of Naples displaced the Spaniards in the early 1700s, and for the next 150 years, the island was handed back and forth among the royal houses of Austria, France and Italy. The British came as allies to the Bourbons in the fight against Napoleon in the 1800s; and after Garibaldi, the unifier of Italy, invaded in 1854 to end the Bourbon rule, Sicily became part of the Italian kingdom in 1861. Now the Germans, in their role of Axis partner, had occupied the island since 1941, and the Sicilians were looking forward once again to liberation, this time by the Americans and British.

Shortly after midnight on July 10, the *Thomas Jefferson* lay a few miles off the southern coast of Sicily, wallowing drunkenly in the heavy seas. The invasion fleet by now numbered over two thousand vessels. Invasion hour had been put off until 2:45 a.m. because of an unexpected Mediterranean storm that whipped wind and waves in uncooperative fury. We had been assembled and waiting in the night blackness at our boat team stations along the rails of the upper decks since midnight. Ordinarily most of us would have been seasick, but the excitement of the moment had our stomachs knotted in controlled spasm, and the anticipation and uncertainty of what lay ahead gripped us all.

The landing hour was again delayed, and then just before four o'clock the PA system droned out its call to the boat teams. We had been due to disembark and go in with the 5th wave, to land one hour after the initial assault, but the storm had thrown all into confusion. Climbing down the wet chain-link nets, we were slapped unmercifully against the side of the transport as it rolled with the heavy swells, but all 15 of us who made up the boat team managed the final hazardous drop into the tossing LCVP safely.

Getting the medical Jeep and trailer into the landing craft with us was almost disastrous. The booms would lower the vehicle to a point above us in the boat where it swung like a demolition ball gone crazy.

We would pull and strain at the hanging guideline that dangled from the Jeep, and then, with the Jeep just over our heads and almost in the boat, the sea would fall away and the line would be ripped from our grasp amid curses and shouts of "Turn it loose!" while the transport rolled one way, the Jeep swung up in another, and our little boat plunged in still another. The next roll of the transport would carry us up and send the Jeep crashing down against our sides or bow as we scrambled to avoid being crushed. After six or seven attempts, the impossible was finally accomplished and, with a sputtering roar of the Diesel motor, we cast loose and headed in the direction of shore.

In all of our practice landings on Cape Cod, Martha's Vineyard, Chesapeake Bay and North Africa, we had hit the right beach only once in eight attempts. We didn't improve our average this time when it was for real. Fortunately, however, as we approached shore, the darkness began to lighten enough that we could see surf pounding against a rocky coast and offshore rocks. It was not at all like the sloping sand beach of the scale relief model we had studied so carefully on board the transport. The fearful bombardment put on by the naval artillery and air support that had raked the beaches an hour before had subsided into an occasional salvo that whistled high above us on its way inland. Since there seemed to be not much activity or small arms fire on the beach itself, we were eventually able to persuade our frightened and obstinate Navy coxswain to swing the boat to port and run parallel to land about a half-mile offshore until we spotted a sandy coastline that seemed more recognizable. Some of the boats in the waves ahead of us had not been so lucky and in the darkness had piled head-on into the offshore rocks. The battalion had lost 45 men by drowning.

In his haste to get us ashore and get back to the safety of the transport area, our uncooperative Navy coxswain rolled down the landing ramp at the first grate of keel on sand. We piled over the sides as the Jeep and trailer shot down the ramp into more than three feet of water. We waded along beside the Jeep, and all went well until the waterproofing gave up in the heavy surf. Our initial surge had covered about 30 yards only. There was still more than one hundred yards ahead to the water's edge. Hip deep in water and with the surf breaking on our backs, we held a brief strategy meeting and decided, in view of the enemy artillery bursts sporadically peppering the shore and shallows, the Jeep and trailer would have to make it on their own.

Once on the beach, we left Corporal Morrow and Red Meier, the Jeep driver, to dig in and keep an eye on the vehicles while the rest of us sought out the access road inland that would lead us to the battalion assembly point. Actually, by our maneuvering offshore, we were within a couple hundred yards of where we should have been. Kenny Prather, the Staff Sergeant in charge of our medical section, scouting on ahead, returned in a few minutes with six happy Sicilian prisoners. They had been manning machine guns in a pillbox nearby and were overjoyed that they had a choice of surrendering to a first-aid kit and a Red Cross armband, rather than to a trigger-happy GI. They had been afraid that they might have had to shoot at someone in self-defense. We turned them over to Morrow and Meier and hiked off to find the battalion.

Allied landing, Gela/Scoglitti, Sicily, July 1943

By noon the battalion had secured its first objectives. Apart from the men lost on landing, there had been few casualties, and we treated these in our first-aid station set up under an olive tree near the Battalion Headquarters. With Sergeant Prather, we walked back to the beach and found that Morrow and Meier, with the aid of the prisoners, had manhandled the Jeep and trailer onto the sandy shore. The motor had dried out and was running again, but when they tried to reach the access road, both Jeep and trailer had bogged down hopelessly up to the tire tops in the soft sand. We all pitched in to dig it out, cleared a path in front of it and sought out the engineer boys who had landed by this time. We borrowed two long rolls of chicken wire, jammed some under the dug-out front and back wheels and laid out the rest in a path in front of the Jeep. When all was set, we lined up on each side of the Jeep and trailer, Meier gunned the engine, and, with a mighty heave and spinning of wheels, we launched the Jeep onto the wire netting. It advanced three yards, but used up all 30 feet of chicken wire, which ended up tightly wound around both front and rear axles.

For the next two hours, while the war swirled around us and the boats kept landing and the shells kept dropping, we took turns under the Jeep with wire clippers, snipping each strand of chicken wire individually and cursing the engineer geniuses. Some time later when the half-tracks rolled ashore, we were pulled out onto firmer ground. Motorized again, we roared off to catch up with the rest of the battalion.

Although we were ignorant of it at the time, we were landing on, fighting on and marching over a site of great antiquity that had seen destruction and sea-borne invasion many times before. On the rocky promontory to our right and on the fertile dunes in front of us, the town of Camerina, founded six hundred years before the birth of Christ, had been destroyed and rebuilt five times before it was eventually abandoned. In 405 B.C., at the time when Syracuse, some 80 miles away on Sicily's eastern coast was the center of Greek civilization and the most powerful city in all Europe, Camerina had been wiped out by an expeditionary landing force of Carthaginians led by the first Hannibal, grandson of Hamilcar. It was rebuilt by Timoleon, destroyed and rebuilt twice in the interval and finally destroyed again by the Romans in 258 B.C. It lingered on as a shell until, during first century B.C., it gradually disappeared forever.

The rocks that form the promontories and line the shores today are not really rocks but fragments of composition building stone, remains of the shattered walls and temples of five Camerinas. Our own modern bombs and explosives had done little damage, the rubble merely disturbed and rearranged by our shelling and returned again to the centuries of nature once we had passed. Today all that remains of a great Greek civilization is a small patch of archeological excavation recently uncovered. All that remain from the brief German occupation are the empty concrete pillboxes overlooking the vulnerable beaches. With the Russian Navy now well established in the Mediterranean, these will probably be put to use again before the century is out.

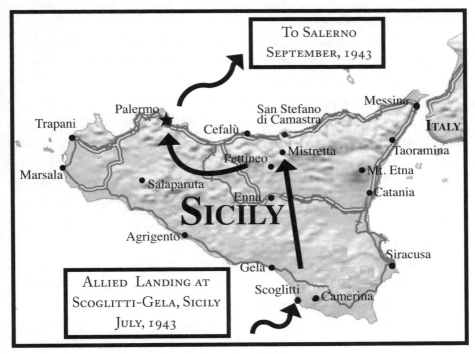

Sicilian Campaign
July - September 1943

Summer 1943: Combat Medicine
Originally published September 1973

IN MID-AUGUST, THE midnight mist rolling in from the sea across one of the few straight stretches of road on the north coast of Sicily was chilling. There were five of us in the Jeep. Meier drove and I sat in the front seat beside him; Watkins, Caronte and Prather were crowded into the back and complaining of the cold. Meier, peering intently ahead into the fog and blackness over the lowered, canvas-covered windshield, was doing his best to make time while dodging potholes and shell craters along the war-torn road. The trailer behind us bounced crazily, loudly rattling its half-load of water cans, litters, splints and plasma boxes.

"I hope the goddamn Krauts are busy up ahead," grunted Watkins between bounces. "Turn on the lights and blow the horn, Meier—maybe they ain't heard us yet."

Beyond the battered two-story shell of a rail station on the left, we dodged a burned-out half-track partially blocking the road. The smell of combat and death still lingered along the debris-strewn highway where only two days before the tanks and tank destroyers had fought a running battle with the retreating Germans. Now, defending a ridge that dropped abruptly to the sea about three miles ahead, the outnumbered Germans had stopped the advance of Patton's entire Seventh Army as it pushed eastward toward Messina.

A half-mile farther on, a guide waving a white handkerchief mounted the road shoulder and flagged us down. He turned us onto a dirt track leading inland toward the dark hills and mountains.

"You guys are late. The rest of the battalion came by over an hour ago."

"It ain't our fault, buddy," said Caronte. "Where the hell is the assembly area?"

"About a mile or two up this road," said the guide, pointing.

"Thanks," grumbled Caronte. "Cap'n, I can smell it already. Another chicken-shit mission."

The broad band of rugged mountains along the entire north coast of Sicily extends inland for more than 30 miles, rising rapidly in places to heights of 6,000 to 7,000 feet. There is a narrow coastal plain in spots, but, for the most part, the main highway and the railroad beside it are chiseled into mountain rock just above the water's edge. The infrequent roads leading southward from the coast hairpin up the mountainsides usually to dead end in some remotely perched town or village high above the sea. In the mountain fastness, only narrow goat and donkey trails, winding in and out along ravines and ridges, connect the isolated villages.

The 157th Infantry's 1st Battalion had been engaging the Germans for two days in a bloody and unsuccessful attempt to push them off the strategic ridge, which met the sea below the mountain town of Motta and Pettineo. East of the ridge was the wide, dry bed of the Mistretta River, and beyond that lay the town of San Stefano di Camastra on the coast. In order to outflank the Germans on the ridge, our 2nd Battalion had been called upon to make a forced march over the inland mountains to the south. To aid in hauling weapons, the ammunition and supplies, the Division's company of mules and muleskinners had been brought up. About one-quarter of the battalion and all of its vehicles had to remain in the rear. Initially, only company medics and litter bearers were to accompany the flanking foot troops, but, at the last minute, someone decided that a group from the aid station should trail the battalion in with extra medical supplies and equipment. As usual (it was early in the European campaign and combat medics had yet to be discovered and glamorized) the orders had reached us belatedly.

By the time we reached the blacked-out assembly area, a barren hilltop of scrub brush, gorse and cactus, it was evident that Caronte's estimate of the situation was correct. The assembly point was deserted except for a couple of supply men.

"We saved you a mule," said one of the supply sergeants.

Sicilian donkeys were at times somewhat uncooperative

"That don't look like no goddamn mule to me," said Watkins, eyeing a tiny, long-eared, moth-eaten Sicilian donkey, which materialized out of the night mist.

"Where the hell is the pack saddle?" asked Prather.

"The heavy weapons boys took the last one."

"How do they expect us to load all this crap?"

"That's your problem."

"Typical! Typical!" said Watkins. "Screw the medics! Always on the short end."

Watkins, a red-faced, balding cynic and semi-reformed alcoholic, had once been chief morgue attendant at Denver General Hospital. Caronte was a short pudgy, comical Brooklyn native who left a job in the Shirley Temple Doll Factory to join the Army. Only Ken Prather, Staff Sergeant in charge of our medical section, was truly at home in the outdoors. In civilian life, Ken had lived on a ranch and herded sheep in the Colorado mountains near the Great Divide. Three years in the Infantry had reinforced his natural silence and preserved a lean hardness.

We unloaded less than half the supplies we'd brought and sent Meier with the Jeep and trailer back to the rear. Using a folded GI blanket as a saddle pad, Prather fashioned some rope slings to drape across the donkey's back. (Caronte had already christened her Angelina in honor, he said, of his stubborn grandmother.) Through the sling loops on each side, we suspended folding litters and a couple of metal-frame leg splints. Several rolls of broad, muslin splint bandage fashioned into a wraparound girth secured this basic load. The rest of the equipment—blankets, plasma boxes, miscellaneous cartons of medical supplies and food rations—was piled on top and tied to the splints and litters with more rope, adhesive tape, muslin and gauze bandage. We roped two five-gallon water cans together and hung these, one on each side for balance, across Angelina's withers. She seemed to tolerate the unholy load, but it took urging to set her into motion. With Prather leading and scouting ahead, Caronte on the halter rope, Watkins and I trailing, we set off into the darkness.

Fourteen hours later, at four in the afternoon, we were still moving, but slowly. Through the night and through the day we had pushed on, up and down hillsides, following ravines, gullies and dried-out streambeds whenever we could; only occasionally had we found a track or path we could use. We proceeded by guess, by map and Prather's compass reading. Three times, on upgrades or downgrades, the load had slipped and we were forced to stop, unpack and reload. It was a lonely, frustrating journey. The war, it seemed, had disappeared. Once or twice during the day, in the distance beyond the mountain ranges between us and the sea, muffled sounds of shooting and artillery fire reached us. Otherwise we were alone in the dusty, deserted, sun-baked countryside, and only the sounds of Angelina's reluctant hooves, the constant creaking of her makeshift load and the clank of water cans broke the silence. It became evident that we were lagging more and more behind the battalion. We had seen none of our own men, and even the few peasant huts we'd passed were empty. The hot Sicilian sun was merciless. By afternoon our sweat-soaked woolen uniforms were stiffly caked with fine, white dust. We had finally reached a terrace of stunted olive and almond trees amid clumps of broad-leafed, prickly pear cactus at the base of the Motta ridge.

"I think Angelina's had it," said Watkins.

"That makes two of us," said Caronte. "My feet are killing me."

"Okay, get her unloaded," said Prather. "We'll give her a rest and cool her off with some water. And we might as well take a chow break ourselves. Maybe in a couple of hours we can get her moving again."

We emptied one of the water cans into our helmets and canteen cups and doused Angelina and ourselves. She refused to eat K-ration dog biscuits but bit off half of a hard chocolate D-bar Caronte held in his hand. He was disgusted. "She's got a sweet tooth just like old Grandma. Jeez! I never thought I'd be playing nursemaid to a butt-headed Sicilian jackass."

"She loves you, Louie," said Watkins. He was sitting, propped against a rock wall, spooning out a can of cold pork and beans and guzzling red wine from one of his two canteens.

Prather and I puzzled over our one field map. "We ought to be about here," said Prather, "and by now the battalion should be over here almost to the coast, behind where the Germans are supposed to be on this ridge."

"At the rate we've been going, it may take us another seven or eight hours to reach them.

"Maybe more," said Prather, watching Watkins who had been hitting the wine all day.

"It still looks like we've got a long climb ahead of us. If we can ever make it to the top of this ridge, we should cross a road that leads inland to Motta."

"Yep. But it runs in the wrong direction. Look," said Prather, "there's a dotted line here which must be one of these cart paths leading off it that loops around to the north again and passes close to the coast about where the battalion should be."

At dusk, for the first time in several hours, the sound of artillery fire started again. It was closer now, but still muffled and far away near the coast. It kept on.

"Somebody's catching it," said Caronte. He waddled over and kicked at Watkins who had snoozed peacefully through it all. "On your feet, Wat. The Krauts are coming."

"Blow it."

"Let's pack up and get moving," said Prather.

We reached the top just past midnight after a tortured nightmare of scrambling. We had zigged and zagged upward, one rock terrace after another in unending succession, some of them barely wide enough to support one row of olive trees or a couple of rows of staked grapevines—Caronte and Prather pulling on Angelina's halter, Watkins and I boosting from the hind end. Twice more on the climb we'd had to stop and repack the load. The road was there on the crest, and it was deserted. We were all exhausted.

"Somebody's gotta be nuts," groaned Caronte. "No goddamn battalion in its right mind ever came this goddamn way."

Prather had walked ahead along the road and returned within a few minutes. He seemed relieved. "I found the cart path. Right where the map said it was. It'll be easy going from now on."

The path took off from the road and headed east about a quarter-mile from where we were. It led along the north slope of a ridge just below the ridge line. Once, in a spot where the mist was thin, a sliver of moon broke through the cloud cover high above and we caught a glimpse of the sea, far below and miles to our left. For the first half-mile the path was smoothly graveled, but it soon changed into a cobblestone surface just wide enough for a narrow animal cart. In places it was bordered by a regular, raised, stone edge; in places, too, wheel ruts, worn deeply into the stone, testified to its antiquity and once heavy use.

Watkins, even though he still nursed a wine hangover, seemed jovial. "If I had more vino, I'd drink a toast to them goddamn old Roman road-builders."

(On a visit to Sicily many years later, I found the road again. Actually, it predated the Romans and once led from the large Sickle-Greek city of Halaesa, which had flourished nearby in 500 B.C. The

Romans may have improved the road during their occupation, but Halaesa itself disappeared around 100 A.D.)

We were moving comfortably now on a gentle downhill grade. The night had darkened and the mist was heavy again. If all went well, we should be reaching the coast in five or six hours.

We came to a stop as Caronte halted Angelina suddenly. "What the hell is that?"

"Sounds like music," said Prather.

We listened intently. Faintly at first, then disappearing completely, then again, waxing and waning, we could hear a thin sound of music. The eerie melody, somewhere in the mist ahead, obviously was on the path and coming toward us as it got progressively louder. Then, only a few yards away, emerging out of the fog, came a peasant leading a small replica of Angelina loaded with straw and a couple of wooden wine casks. He was playing a concertina. When he stopped, he was almost on us. It was hard to tell who was more surprised. He was a small, weathered man, dressed in typical peasant fashion, wearing dusty, frayed trousers, a shapeless cap on his head and a nondescript, dark woolen coat draped over the shoulders of a dirty, open-necked shirt of coarse cloth.

Watkins was first to react. "Speak to him in Wop, Caronte. Ask him what in the hell he's doing out here on this God-forsaken mountain at two a.m. Don't he know there's a war going on?"

After the initial surprise, our peasant friend seemed entirely at ease. Caronte tried out his best pidgin, Brooklynese Italian. The peasant answered in an almost unrecognizable Sicilian dialect. There was a lot of hand waving and good fellowship. I could pick up only a word or two.

"You don't have to kiss him, Louie," said Watkins. "What's he telling you?"

"He says his name is Giuseppe—Joe—Mazzara, and he's on his way home. He's got a cousin in Yonkers."

"Jesus," said Watkins. "They all got cousins somewhere."

"He says the Germans pulled out yesterday."

The peasant nodded vigorously. He brushed one open palm quickly and dramatically against the other in the direction of east. "Tedeschi, Tutti scappati!"

"That's what they always say," said Prather.

"Caronte," said Watkins, eyeing the two wine casks, "you're a lousy intelligence corporal. Find out if he's interested in trading us some wine for cigarettes."

The peasant grinned. "Americani? Buono."

Watkins tapped on one of the casks, held a couple of empty canteens upside down and conveyed the message adequately in sign language and two words: "Vino? Cigaretti?"

After filling Watkins's canteens, Mazzara insisted that the rest of us take some too. The wine was harsh and sour, but warming. After a round of drinking, the peasant struck a small wax match and lit one of his bartered cigarettes. A few minutes later we broke up the party. He waved goodbye and continued up the trail with his donkey; we moved on in the opposite direction. The concertina music began again, and, just before it faded away in the distance behind us, he must have stopped to light another cigarette. The mist had cleared somewhat and the reflection of the match flare, even from a great distance, shone like a beacon.

"That's one bastard who never heard of a blackout," grumbled Watkins.

A minute later the first shell exploded near the trail about a hundred yards to our rear. Six or seven more, all hitting on the ridge or near the cart path followed it. The brief warning whistles were unmistakable.

"Mortars," yelled Prather. "Let's get off this road."

We scrambled down about three levels onto a terraced grape vineyard and sought protection along a low rock wall. Another barrage of mortar bursts came whistling in, exploding along the trail we'd left. A third barrage followed, and then all was quiet.

"I knew there was something phony about that character," said Watkins. "I bet he was a goddamn German agent infiltrating the lines. He must have had a walkie-talkie with him and spotted us for the Krauts."

"You're so smart," said Caronte. "Why the hell didn't you challenge him?"

"With what? A 5cc syringe?"

"You could have poked around in that straw while he was dealing out the wine."

"Yeah. And supposin' he had a burp gun slung under that baggy coat. Where would we be?"

"Nuts," said Prather. "Knock it off. The shooting's over."

We decided to abandon the path and stay put where we were for the rest of the night. Angelina was unloaded again, and we tied her halter rope to a vine stake nearby. We stretched out on the rocky ground along the wall and went to sleep under some dusty grapevines.

Suddenly, it was morning and broad daylight. Caronte was shaking my arm.

"Cap'n. Wake up. The donkey's gone and so is Prather."

"Where's Wat?"

"Still passed out under the grapevines. He finished off the wine and a pint of grain alcohol last night before he went to sleep."

"Well, see if you can revive him. I'll heat up some water for coffee. We'll eat breakfast and wait here for Kenny. He'll be back."

It was an hour later when we spotted Prather heading our way on the trail above. He was leading Angelina. She had pulled loose during the night and wandered off, dragging stake and grapevine at the end of her halter rope. Prather found her about a half-mile away nibbling on cactus leaves. After tying her up temporarily, he had gone ahead on the trail for a couple of miles and run into a squad from H Company.

"They were pulling out and heading toward the coast to rejoin the battalion," said Prather.

"Did they have any casualties?" asked Caronte, still thinking about the shelling a few hours before.

"Nope. One guy had a headache and wanted some APCs."

And what the hell were they doing last night while the Krauts were shelling bejeesus out of us?" asked Watkins.

Prather grimaced. "According to the way they told it, they spotted some lights and activity on this ridge last night and blasted the hell out of a whole company of Germans."

"Holy tomato! And I could've stayed in Brooklyn making dolls," said Caronte. "Well, anyway, I'm glad them heroes are a bunch of lousy mortar men."

We reloaded Angelina and started on our way again. Within three hours we had reached the coast, still looking for the battalion. There was traffic now on the coast road. A Jeep and trailer approaching us from the direction of the front looked familiar. Prather was up on the road flagging it. It was Meier.

"Where have you guys been?" he asked. "I've been up and down this road for the past two hours looking for you."

"What's going on?" asked Prather.

"Nothing, now. The Germans pulled out yesterday afternoon, and they moved the rest of us up the coast road last night," said Meier. "A couple of platoons from G Company are already across the river and into San Stefano."

"Did the battalion trap any Germans?"

"Naw. They were long gone before our guys even reached the coast."

"Where's the battalion now?"

"Up ahead," said Meier, "sitting on their duffs. We been ordered to hold. There's a big rumor that the whole division is gonna be relieved. We're waiting for the 3rd Division to move through us this afternoon."

"My achin' back," said Watkins, aiming a kick at Angelina's scrawny rump.

Caronte climbed into the Jeep, pulled off his shoes and began massaging his feet. "What a chicken-shit war."

Blake: Permanent Second Lieutenant
Originally published August 1977

This is the story of Blake, Jack Blumberg, an old friend from the days of that war going on in Europe 34 years ago. We have tried to write about him before, but always without success. He wasn't a difficult person to know; in fact, almost everyone who had any dealings with him soon became devoted to his charm, his kindness and his unfailing cheerfulness. Yet his personality had many facets that often confused description. He mystified many, who considered him a "screwball"; he provoked many, who often shook their heads and muttered, "That goddamned Blumberg." He confounded many, who worried and said, "Oh Jesus! Blake's in trouble again." But no one who knew him ever disliked him. He was a free spirit in a time when there wasn't much to be lighthearted about.

By the time late August had rolled around in 1943, we had known Blake nearly a year and a half. By that time, too, the Sicilian campaign had ended and the 157th Infantry Regiment was in bivouac on the north coast of Sicily. General Montgomery and the British and Canadian troops of his Eighth Army were busy at the far eastern end of the island preparing to cross over into Italy and continue chasing the Germans. For General Patton's American Seventh Army, the fighting was over. We were back in a rest area, and our 2nd Battalion aid station was comfortably situated in a grove of ancient olive trees on a hillside overlooking the peaceful, blue Mediterranean, about midway between the cities of Palermo, 30 miles to the west, and Cefalù to the east. We use the phrase "comfortably situated" reservedly. At least we were stationary, no one was shooting at us, and, for the first time, we were able to shed the dusty woolen clothes we had lived in for weeks. The kitchen units were functioning (also for the first time) K- and C-rations were forgotten temporarily, and we were eating three prepared meals a day, sitting at a makeshift, wooden-trestle table in the shade of the olive trees.

Jack "Blake" Blumberg

The weather remained hot and dry, but the burning, daylight sunshine was tempered by a constant sea breeze, which also brought a pleasant chill to the nights. We had set up our aid-station tent for the first time, and the men had paired off into their shelter-half tents; most of us, however, still preferred to sleep in the open on top of our bedding rolls and sleeping bags under a tent of mosquito netting. The mosquitoes weren't bad in our location, but the flies were plentiful and ferocious. We had captured an Italian officer's field bathtub, a flimsy aluminum affair tacked onto a board base. It leaked alarmingly around the nail holes attaching it to the wood, but with someone pouring water into the perforated tin-can shower-head that hung from an olive branch, it was a joy to bathe standing on something smooth and clean again instead of bare, rocky soil. After showering, we used the accumulated soapy water in the tub to wash clothes.

Apart from the daily visitors who came by regularly for minor medical treatment or conversation, we had a small chummy group who made our luxurious, aid-station, country-club area its home—Abba Messe, the Assistant Battalion Surgeon; Jack Weiner, the Battalion Intelligence Officer; George Viereck, Weiner's Intelligence Corporal; Bill Galvin, the Regimental Intelligence Officer; and Blake. We joined in the softball and volleyball games, we played bridge and gin rummy, we drank lemon-powder drink spiked with grain alcohol, we laughed at Weiner's Yiddish stories and we talked endlessly. Most of all we loved to get Blake started on stories.

Blake was undoubtedly the star of our gathering. He had been born in Reading, Pennsylvania, the younger of two sons of a wealthy manufacturing family. His parents had died young, and his upbringing and education had been taken over by a devoted brother. His four years of secondary schooling were spent at New York Military Academy, and he had just graduated from the University of Pennsylvania when he was drafted into the Army. He had attended OCS at Fort Ord in California and then joined the 45th Division as a second lieutenant in the spring of 1942. In his time with the Regiment, he had been shunted around into every conceivable job that a shavetail could hold and had remained unpromoted. He was known as an incorrigible goof-off—a permanent second lieutenant.

Blake was extremely intelligent and willing. It was just his complete unconcern with the thousand petty annoyances and obligations of military service and his complete disregard of time and punctuality that kept him in constant hot water with the brass. We knew his story by heart: after four years of model behavior during the regimented life at New York Military Academy, where every hour of every day was scheduled down to the fraction of a minute, on the day of graduation he threw away his watch and vowed never to look at another timepiece again. He had coasted through the University of Pennsylvania in unscheduled, happy-go-lucky fashion and, somehow, had gotten through officer's school in the same manner. He had survived, with no change of habit, more than a year of stateside training with the Division. He saw no reason to alter his philosophy then, and, actually, the free and easy life of real combat suited him best of all.

Blake was neat, trimly built, dark-haired, quite handsome and extremely attractive, especially to women. We had watched and marveled at his exploits during weekend leaves on the streets of New York, Boston, Worcester, Richmond and wherever. In the middle of a sightseeing stroll down the streets of a strange city, if a particularly beautiful girl passed by and caught his fancy, he would turn abruptly on his heel, pursue, discreetly engage her in conversation, bring her back to the strolling group, introduce her pleasantly as a long lost friend or cousin, borrow the key to someone's hotel room and have her in bed all within a few minutes. Sometimes he might join us again later in the day, but more often he would only reappear back in camp on a Monday morning, four hours late again for duty. We didn't doubt at all his California stories about Hollywood and young starlets, nor did we dispute his claim to be a cousin of Prince Mike Romanoff, the outlandishly phony Russian nobleman (a renegade Blumberg, according to Blake) who intimidated movie industry moguls. We figured Blake's *chutzpah* came naturally. In combat, most of us never even caught a glimpse of a Sicilian Signorina. Blake invariably located the village beauty, the mayor's niece, the local Duke's daughter or even a lonesome Countess. Most of the rest of us were dull, overly inhibited and married. We lived vicariously through Blake.

Nothing bothered Blake; nothing fazed him. He was always smiling, always cheerful, always nonchalant. *Toujours gai.* He played at soldiering like an actor—a dashing combination of Douglas Fairbanks Sr. and Jr., John Wayne, Ronald Coleman, Errol Flynn, Lord Mountbatten and Lawrence of Arabia. It was his perfect imitation of that incomparable paragon of military competence, Sergeant Blake of the Army Training films, that earned him the name by which he was generally known. Many years after the war, on seeing the slim and youthful Sergeant Blake when he first appeared in the movies, the manner and physical likeness were so striking that it was hard to believe it wasn't Blake himself.

Blake was also terribly nearsighted. Without glasses he could see nothing but a blur of forms and faces. In spite of this handicap, in earlier years, he had been the New York State Golden Gloves boxing champion of his weight class. In combat, his nearsightedness did occasionally create problems, mostly hilarious ones. Like the time he misread a signpost and directed his driver, "Legs," onto a dusty road and followed a retreating column of German supply trucks for miles into enemy territory. Or the time on a night mission with a patrol from his platoon when, crouching behind a rock wall, he heard and thought he saw a squad of Germans approaching and gave the order to fire. When the shooting stopped he discovered a dead white Italian cow. Nonplussed, Blake had the men skin and quarter the animal, and hauled the meat back to the platoon for a barbecue breakfast.

It was in Italy, more than a month later, after we had pushed out of the Salerno beachhead and were moving up toward Avellino, that we heard the news about Blake. He had been transferred into the 3rd Battalion's I Company, still a second lieutenant and still leading patrols. A German sniper's bullet had killed him. Someone brought his steel-rimmed spectacles and helmet back to our aid station. We didn't know what to do with them. The glasses were shattered, and there was a neat hole almost directly through the gold, Second Lieutenant's bar welded to the front of his helmet.

September 1943: On to Salerno
Originally published September 1968

B Y THE FIRST week in September, the Sicilian campaign was over. The 157th Regiment was bivouacked under some ancient olive trees on a rocky hillside along the north coast of Sicily, overlooking the beautiful, blue Mediterranean. For the first time since the invasion landing almost four weeks earlier, we had set up our aid-station tent (small, wall, one each) and were enjoying some of those leisure hours that punctuate the lives of combat troops and afford opportunity to swap and embellish the wild tales and experiences that accumulate during any action. There is an exhilarating sensitivity and poignant humor among men of the front line that can never be communicated adequately to those who don't "belong," even those of the same regiment or division who may be one or more echelons to the rear. In light of the months that were to follow, we were mere novices at the time, but already we considered ourselves combat veterans and were well pleased with our soldiering capabilities.

Much of the heavy fighting during the Sicilian campaign took place in the broad and mountainous eastern third of the island. The tactical plan of the German occupation forces (who were greatly outnumbered by the invading British, Canadian and American divisions) was to abandon Sicily and fight a delaying action while their troops withdrew to Messina at the northeast corner where they could cross the narrow strait between the Charybdis and Scylla of Greek mythology onto the toe and mainland of Italy. The Germans were well trained and competent, many of them veteran troops of the Afrika Corps; they did not get much help from the local Sicilian homeguard or their allied Italian troops who, by this time, had little appetite for fighting and offered resistance only when German guns were at their backs. The British and Canadians, landing to the east of the Americans, had the most difficult task as they pushed straight northward toward Mt. Etna and the pivotal area of the German holding defense.

Meanwhile to the west, the American divisions fanned out and sped northward through the central portion of the island, covering great distances and encountering only brief pockets of rearguard German resistance. Our race was for the north coast road at mid-island in the hope of isolating the German forces around Palermo and the western sector before they could be withdrawn toward Messina.

But nearly always, and with masterful skill, the Germans were a few hours and one or two steps ahead of us.

As a result, for the American forces at least, the campaign was one of rapid motion and pursuit. It was an ideal initiation into combat for the 45th Division and our eager 157th. During the first three days the Regiment earned its spurs and the respect of the higher command by successfully taking the strongly held inland mountain towns of Vizzini and Grammichele and by capturing a major airfield at Comiso where the garrison was taken by surprise and 120 planes, most of them fighters, were destroyed on the ground. After that there was just enough action—brief engagements against small defensive units of capable Germans employing mortar and small arms fire, encounters with the shelling of the mobile and efficient, all-purpose 88s in every strategic village and at every road junction, booby traps, roadblocks and blown bridges, and some occasional strafing by the still active Luftwaffe—to let us know we were actually engaged in war and not another training maneuver. At the same time the relative ease and success of our rapid advances built up some needed confidence.

Our 2nd Battalion encountered its heaviest fighting on reaching the north coast where, spearheading a pre-dawn Division advance, we surprised (or were surprised by) a rearguard company of the enemy who pinned us down for three hours in a brisk battle. There, really for the first time, we experienced the acute anxiety of administering plasma and morphine by the light of a burning Jeep and treating casualties where they lay on open hillsides amid mortar bursts and fire from automatic weapons. On another unforgettable night, four of us from the aid station trailed the battalion, as it made an inland flanking maneuver on foot, crosscountry over a series of mountain ridges to the south of where the 1st Battalion was having a bitter three-day battle on the coast. There we encountered our greatest trial in the form of two, long-eared, gray Sicilian donkeys, which we had heavily and inexpertly laden with water cans, splints, litters and medical supplies. The reluctant animals understood no English and had to be nursed every inch of the way up and down the terraced hillsides, over rocky ridges and into winding gullies and ravines. On the steep downhill slopes, the loads, held in place by ropes and muslin bandages, would tumble over their heads and, on the uphill scrambles, slide back over their rumps. It was a lonely trek; we proceeded by compass, by guess and by following the spoor of D-bar wrappings and discarded K-ration dog biscuits. The flanking maneuver was successful, but it was two days before its worn out medical support caught up with the battalion. At San Stefano, on the coast, just as the Division was being relieved for the first time by the 3rd Division, our G Company got badly mangled crossing a heavily mined, dry riverbed.

When the call for more help came, we loaded a commandeered bicycle with plasma and medical supplies, rode forward to the near end of the blown bridge, and, in sublime ignorance, stumbled across two hundred yards of uncleared minefield to reach the wounded on the far side. Later, after the engineers had cleared a path through the riverbed, the 3rd Division moved through, tripped six more mines along the path and suffered eighteen more casualties. The Regiment was called on one more time, near the end of the campaign, to make another flanking maneuver, this time by sea along the north coast. We landed just short of Messina, but again the Germans had pulled out ahead of us. The 3rd Division was not happy with us. On landing in darkness, we cut all their communication lines and fouled up their water supply. With the fighting over, as we rode back through the villages and towns along the north coast, the friendly Sicilians (almost everyone had a relative somewhere in America) would come out of hiding, line the streets and hang from windows to cheer us and present us with gifts, flowers, fruit and wine.

This had it all over maneuvers in the States. If this is what combat was like, we were all for it. We felt confident and invincible.

At that time the medical section of an infantry battalion consisted of a Battalion Surgeon, an Assistant Battalion Surgeon and 36 enlisted men headed by a Staff Sergeant. As far as the two doctors were concerned, it was a flagrant waste of medical talent—if you could call our few years of post-medical-school training that. A junior medical student or one of our well-trained tech sergeants could have carried out the duties of both doctors just as efficiently and almost as intelligently. The conditions we encountered during those first weeks of combat resembled little for which the training of the years before had prepared us. On maneuvers, the aid station was always neatly laid out somewhere to the rear of Battalion Headquarters, with its tent set up and medical chests opened; its areas conveniently marked off for reception, screening, medical, walking-wounded, litter-wounded; and its Lister Bag filled with water and hanging from its tripod.

During the weeks of action, practically none of the medical equipment ever got unpacked. All treatment was given on the run, and we practiced mainly from the medical kits hanging from our webbing belts, and out of the two dust-covered Jeep trailers parked along the roadsides, under the olive and almond trees, behind the prickly-pear cactuses and rock fences, or in farmyards. In the first thirteen days we covered over three hundred circuitous miles reaching the north coast. We were constantly on the move, seldom spending more than a few hours in any one place, sleeping in the open, or in some cleared out corner of a deserted peasant hut. The steady, unrelieved monotony of three food-concentrate meals a day out of K-ration boxes and C-ration cans, combined with the physical exertion, effectively eliminated all bowel activity, and it was not until we reached the fertile north coast with its abundant vineyards and fruit orchards that the diarrheas set in.

The two-week respite in early September gave us a chance to discard about one quarter of our medical equipment and reorganize the rest. We acquired another standard Jeep (a replacement for the underpowered amphibian 1/4-ton that pulled one of the trailers) and an unauthorized 3/4-ton, which we were able to load with extra water cans and much of the heavy equipment and which provided needed transportation for the litter bearers and aid-station personnel. Ab Messe, our Assistant Battalion Surgeon, was a compulsive consolidator, and whenever the opportunity presented, more and more of the outmoded and infrequently used equipment was left behind. We had "liberated" a 1900 vintage microscope somewhere along the way, and in the bivouac area, with some borrowed slides and stain, we amused ourselves making blood smears and slides of stool specimens. But after two weeks of diligent searching and turning up not one malaria plasmodium or one parasite egg, we finally gave up trying to practice scientific medicine and reverted to the clinical pragmatism of sulfanilamide, APC and paregoric. The microscope was "consolidated out" on the next move.

Our most valued acquired possession, however, was a captured Italian officer's aluminum bathtub. Everyone develops his own methods of bathing under field conditions, particularly where water is a scarce commodity. Standing in the bathtub instead of on the bare dirt we perfected the technique of a complete bath using only one canteen cup of warm water having enough left over to brew coffee and, after two or three of us had gone through the same procedure, using the soapy water that had accumulated in the tub to do laundry in. We carried the tub with us for another two months. It finally became so battered, leaky and unusable that it had to go. Even then, we swapped it to an Italian peasant in the mountains near Cassino for two chickens, three tomatoes and a bottle of wine.

On September 10, the U.S. 5th Army invaded Italy, landing on the beaches south of Salerno. Within a few days of the landing, the 45th Division was again called on. The tent had to be folded and packed away, and we moved once more to a staging area, this time on the outskirts of Palermo. There we awaited the hard-working Navy LCIs shuttling between Sicily and Italy and another trip by sea to land us on that beleaguered beachhead.

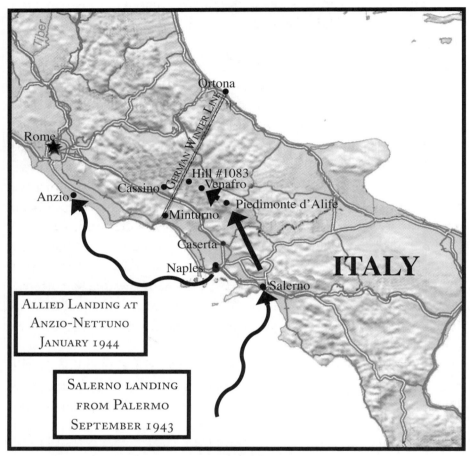

Italian Campaign: Salerno – Venafro – Anzio
September 1943 – February 1944

September 1943: Jack Weiner
Originally published September 1963

T WENTY YEARS AGO almost to the day, we were sitting against a wall in the noonday sun fanning Mediterranean flies out of a C-ration can of pork and beans. Stretched out next to us was a good friend, Jack Weiner, our Battalion S-2, feeling feverish and miserable. We were waiting, along with the rest of the battalion, for the trucks to pick us up and take us to the docks in Palermo harbor.

The art of medical diagnosis does not flourish in a hot sun within the walled confines of a bare and smelly goat yard. Weiner had a temperature over 102° and was vomiting at intervals, but he wouldn't go to the hospital. He didn't want to miss the boat trip to Salerno. A few days later we were side by side again in a shell hole on the beachhead dodging mortar bursts. Weiner had turned yellow as a pumpkin, and the diagnosis became obvious. By this time he was too sick to argue.

Salerno: Allied troop landing, September 1943

It seems strange now that an ailing but intelligent man could want to pass up a legitimate chance to avoid a combat landing where he might get himself killed. But that was the way it was then. If you were in the dusty, walking infantry, the prospect of a shower, food served to you at a real table, a night or two in a Navy bunk and a sea-going boat trip, even on an LCL, seemed like a vacation cruise on a luxury yacht. Besides, after you had been through combat with an outfit, it was home and you didn't want to risk the hospital, replacement depot, reassignment shuffle that might drop you into some cruddy unit.

Weiner spent the next two months in North Africa, hospitalized with the hepatitis. He finally went AWOL, bummed a ride to Naples by air, stole a Jeep and drove 60 kilometers in the rain to rejoin the battalion. Just before he reached us, the Jeep skidded into a ditch, turned over and fractured a couple of his ribs. This flared up the hepatitis again and about two years later, when Weiner eventually made it out of the hospitals on his own power, the war was over. War may never be so pleasant again.

Fall 1943: Piedimonte d'Alife
Originally published November 1968

PIEDIMONTE D'ALIFE LIES against the lower slope of Italy's Matese range in the central Apennines between Naples and Rome. Like hundreds of other small mountain towns, its narrow streets and stone houses have remained almost unchanged since the early Middle Ages. Today, reflecting the general prosperity of the last two decades, a two-or-three-block-wide perimeter of modern four-and-five-story family apartments partially rings the southern edge away from the steeper hills. But the central core remains the same even to the cobbled streets, the decaying ducal palace and the community troughs where the women still do their laundry by hand, exchange gossip and invective and look suspiciously on strangers.

When our 2nd Battalion captured Piedimonte in mid-October 1943, about one-half of the town was in shambles. It had been shelled heavily by our artillery; the Germans, as they pulled out, blew up bridges, utility installations and anything else that might be of possible use to us; after our arrival it was battered once more by the German artillery. This, of course, is the standard pattern in any combat area and is the unfortunate fate of any innocent civilian population caught between advancing and retreating armies.

We had come a long way, in both distance and experience, since landing on the Italian mainland. It had soon become evident that the Italian campaign was not to be the fast-moving affair we had enjoyed in Sicily. It was also evident that the leadership of the American Fifth Army (by command, always identified in press releases as "General Mark Clark's Fifth Army") lacked the imagination and purpose of the Seventh Army under Patton. Things were just confused, and stayed that way. The fight for the Salerno beachhead revealed that the Germans did not intend to write off Italy as they had Sicily, and the near-disaster there was averted only by some determined and makeshift scrambling on the part of General Middleton, Colonel Ankcorn and their 45th Division troops. Even after our breakout, the Germans retreated slowly and according to plan, awaiting the fall rains and the preparation of their first winter defense line in the rugged mountains south of Rome. We seemed to stumble along after them in uncoordinated fashion, advancing when we should have been regrouping and holding when we should have been advancing.

Our battalion was the last unit to leave Sicily. We arrived in the bay south of Salerno off Paestum four days after the initial landing when the fighting on shore was reaching its peak. For 48 hours we constituted the entire "floating reserve" of General Clark's whole Fifth Army. We disembarked, finally, one afternoon under full German observation and marched off in one direction to an assembly area behind the British and Colonel Darby's Rangers. During the night we moved again back to the beach, and, by daylight and again in full view, we marched out in another direction. In the next 36 hours we shuttled twice more on similar moves. This, we learned later, was to impress the enemy that a continuous flow of fighting men was pouring onto the beachhead. If the Germans were taken in by the deception, they gave no immediate signs of being intimidated.

By September 18, having failed in their attempt to dislodge the landing forces, the Germans began to withdraw into the surrounding mountains. Along with the 3rd Division, which had just landed, and as one of the few "fresh" units available, our 2nd Battalion was given the task of pushing inland out of the beachhead in pursuit of the retreating enemy. We moved through Battipaglia, a town totally destroyed in which each single building had been reduced to flat, dusty rubble. Eboli (where Christ stopped in the story by Carlo Levi), a few miles away, was almost as badly devastated. Above Eboli, at the dead end of a winding mountain road in an oppressive cul-de-sac between ridges, we liberated the village of Campagna, which had been used as an internment camp for political prisoners. There, huddled together in miserable squalor, we found almost a thousand civilians from Southern and Eastern Europe, most of them Jews.

It was a strange experience to be surrounded by a weeping, clamorous crush of cadaverous humans whose gratitude was overwhelming and whose needs and hunger were so acute. We gave away all of our rations and extra supplies. We called in the medical group from Regiment and set up an infirmary and hospital of sorts and began treating the critically ill with what we had. It was not much, and we could do little. Our sense of inadequacy was magnified by the impressive and overpowering, combined intellect of our patients among whom were university regents, doctors of philosophy, full professors and some of the foremost medical clinicians of Europe. When we had to move on the next day, the Division arranged for a field hospital unit to take over.

The rainy season began early that year and, from the first week in October on, heavy and intermittent downpours kept us soaked and uncomfortable. By necessity we became expert in putting up the aid-station tent. On any spot where we thought we might spend a night or linger more than a few hours, the tent was out of the trailer, up and staked down within three minutes. The fighting had steadily increased and contacts and engagements with enemy troops were daily occurrences. The war had become a lot more personal too. Many of the old aid-station visitors who used to gather frequently during the lulls in action for conversation, coffee, and hot lemon drink spiked with grain alcohol were missing now. Jack Weiner, evacuated at Salerno, was in serious condition with hepatitis at a base hospital in Tunisia. The irrepressible Blumberg, permanent second lieutenant, was killed by a sniper's bullet through the forehead while leading a night patrol near Oliveto. Colonel Ankcorn, our wonderful Regimental Commander, had lost a leg when his Jeep ran over a road mine near Valva. Two of our own aid men had been wounded in the fighting at Sant' Angelo.

Late one afternoon, on the road between Ponte and Guardia, we loaded one of the Jeeps with empty water cans and sent both drivers, Red Meier and Daffy Martinez, back with it to the nearest water point. We were behind a stone building just below the road at the time, and as they pulled out, an 88 shell hit. When we all rushed up to help move them and the Jeep off the road, another shell hit the embankment to our right, scattering rock and dust, and rolled down on the road beside us, unexploded. We had already learned to be grateful to those unsung saboteurs in the German munitions works who managed to slip in one dud for every eight shells. But Meier, with a tiny penetrating wound of the chest, died without regaining consciousness. The fragment that hit Martinez ripped away both eyes.

Allied troops disarm German shell that failed to detonate

On October 19 we were in Piedimonte d'Alife. After 40 days of continuous combat, our occupation of the town signaled the first break in the campaign for us. The 45th Division, moving up the mountainous central core of the peninsula, was pinched out between the 34th Division on the left and the British Eighth Army on the right. The 157th Regiment pulled back from Piedimonte to the village of San Potito less than two miles away and went into reserve for a two-week period of rest, reoutfitting and training of new replacements.

As the fighting pressed onward toward the Volturno River north of us, it was pleasant to be left behind in the quiet countryside, now well beyond range of enemy artillery. We cleaned up, loafed and slept. The mail caught up with us. The field kitchens were brought up and put into operation for the first time since landing. The hot meals were welcome. After six weeks on K- and C-rations, no matter how well doctored by individual enterprise and ingenuity, food from an army field kitchen, even served in an aluminum mess kit, is a treat.

There was always a gathering of ragged, hungry children standing by silently and hopefully near the chow lines. One of the regulars, a quiet, large-eyed, 14-year-old, Severino d'Andrea, adopted our aid-station group. Severino, too proud to beg and too honorable to steal, became a favorite. Every evening, having loaded him with more canned rations, shoes, clothes and odds and ends than he could carry, we sent him off on foot to his home in Piedimonte. A special few of us had the good luck to be invited on several occasions into Piedimonte for a meal with Severino's family. Mama d'Andrea, with some army flour, a few cans of C-rations plus an occasional rabbit or chicken and whatever fruits, vegetables, greens and wine Severino could turn up on his daily trading and scrounging jaunts around the town and nearby farms, would turn out a seven-course meal that staggered the imagination.

Last fall, after an interval of 24 years, we revisited Piedimonte d'Alife and San Potito. We found the farmyard and the olive tree where the aid-station tent was pitched. We found Severino now married and with two young children of his own. He is the Professor of Language at the Scuola Media, the newly built, town high school, and one of the town's leading citizens. His two sisters and one brother-in-law also are teachers; his young brother, just back from Argentina, owns a television and appliance store. Papa d'Andrea is retired and gives free advice to the children. The family built one of the new modern apartments, and they are all there, the appliance store on the first floor with an apartment for Papa and the rest in layers above, each family with a floor of its own. Only Mama is gone. But her cooking talent remains with the daughters. On short notice, with help from all floors, they produced a ten-course meal that staggered us again. From the balcony of Severino's apartment on the top floor you can see all of Piedimonte. It lies quietly against the foothills, and, except for a pockmarked building here and there, you might never know it had been through a war.

Christmas 1943
Originally published December 1968

B Y THE WEEK before Christmas in 1943, we had become so familiar with the narrow rocky trail that led down from the mountain church to the regimental area in the olive groves on the lower slopes east of Venafro that we could negotiate it, even in darkness, in just under three hours. Since November 8, when we had come out of reserve and returned to action on the mountainous front between Cassino and Venafro where we encountered the first German line of winter defense, we had advanced not at all. The repetitive pattern of eight days up in the front-line positions, four days back in the regimental area for rest, eight days on the line again, became a monotonous routine.

There was nothing sunny about Italy that fall. The weather grew increasingly cold; the dreary skies were dark and heavy with clouds, the fogs and mists hung at treetop level. The incessant rains had turned the lower terraces and the entire Volturno valley stretching out behind us into a sea of water and mud. After six weeks, the tent area under the dripping olive trees had been churned into a sodden quagmire. The damp, murky air was permeated with the odors of wet woolen clothing; refuse from the field kitchens and seepage from the pit latrines. The line of 105 howitzers immediately behind us boomed steadily through the days and nights, looping barrage after barrage over the mountaintops, adding the acrid smell of burnt powder. There was not much rest in the rest area, and by the end of four days we were always eager to shoulder our pack boards and make the arduous six-hour climb up the trail to the relative comfort of the front line.

The war had settled into a standoff of sending out patrols, occasionally probing for weakness in platoon strength, and the constant dueling between the long range artilleries. In the mountains, the German defenses were thinly held but exceedingly well prepared and located.

At many places along the line, enemy positions were within 50 to 100 yards of our own. Each side played its own little game of "shoot at me and I'll shoot at you"; every burst of mortar shells brought an answering volley. And overhead, the intermittent whistling of heavy artillery shells passed back and forth, day and night, seeking out the installations and troop concentrations behind both lines.

La Chiesa di Madonna della Fondata, aid station, Hill #1083

We had put the aid station in a small, isolated church, La Chiesa di Madonna della Fondata, built partially into the side of a rocky hill and on a narrow ledge overhanging a deep gorge. It was the only structure of substance in the entire area, and you could follow the footpaths that led to it for miles in any direction without seeing a sign of habitation. It was not an ideal location, since it was directly on the front line between the positions of our F and G Companies. Three hundred yards to our rear, on the reverse slope of the bald hilltop that lay between us, was Battalion Headquarters, operating out of a thatch and stone goat pen. Ordinarily, as medics, we would have been outranked and denied the use of any such comfortable shelter, but during our first days there we soon learned the reason why no one else chose it.

The cream-colored walls and red tiled roof of our little chapel perched on its high ledge stood out like a red-and-white bull's-eye against the background of green hillsides. We were in direct view of the German positions dug into the higher slopes beyond the gorge, and less than four hundred yards away. Although we displayed no Geneva Cross, the Germans seemed to be aware that we were using the church as a medical aid station. We had to play by their rules, however. We could move about on the outside freely only in darkness at night or when the fogs and rain obscured visibility. If more than one person ever ventured out in daylight, or if we attempted to carry out a litter case, they would bracket the church with their deadly accurate 88 shells, one short, one long, one below and one above. Occasionally when they felt playful, they would clip a tile off the roof ridge, or chip away at the corner of the rock ledge.

Except when there was a platoon or company skirmish, or an unusual amount of patrol activity, we seldom had to treat more than two or three wounded each day. As the weeks went on, however, our casualty rate from exposure, frostbite and "trench foot" grew in alarming amounts. It became a source of much bitterness to learn that the new combat boots, shoe packs, combat suits and cold weather gear had reached the Italian Theater weeks before and were being worn 30 and 40 miles behind the lines in Caserta and Naples. We were still dressed in regular wool issue clothing, canvas leggings and GI shoes. None of the new protective clothing reached us until the last days of December. Some nights as many as eight or ten men had to be carried into the church. It often required four and five grains of morphine to relieve their intense pain.

The evacuation of our litter cases remained a nightmare. The closest Jeep or ambulance was miles away in the regimental area at the base of the mountains. We had tried several kinds of litter rigs attached to the backs of the pack mules that brought up supplies, but all proved impractical. The mountain trails were too jagged and narrow, and the jolting and swaying as the animals climbed and descended the slippery paths often compounded injuries or threw the patients into shock. We had to settle for the laborious and frustratingly slow method of hand carrying. Nine litter relay stations were set up on the trail between Battalion Headquarters and the vehicle pool at the mountain base. As it was an impossible job for two men, each litter required a team of four litter bearers. It took between five and six hours to move one litter case from the church to an ambulance.

Bucky Behers and Dr. Graff

We were in a discouraged frame of mind coming down off the mountain just five days before Christmas. Colonel Knight, our taciturn commanding officer, sensing our apathy, suggested an impromptu three-day leave. We needed no urging. Neither did our new driver, Bucky Behers, who was more than anxious to put the Jeep in use again. All of 19 years old, Bucky was one of those earnest people whose eagerness to please was exceeded only by his overdeveloped compassion. By the time we left, he had a list of things to pick up from every man in the medical section.

We reached Naples in mid-afternoon after a wild, wet ride. We found Lee Powers, one of the medical officers who had left the regiment after Sicily, and moved our sleeping bags into his apartment quarters near the harbor. Lee took us to a restaurant and fed us a real meal. Afterwards he got us tickets to a USO performance at the old San Carlo Opera.

As we sat warm and comfortably relaxed in the red plush seats and opulent surroundings, we were overcome by fatigue and a frightening sense of unreality. It was a disturbing experience. Less than three hours away, on the mountain, shells were dropping, shrapnel fragments flying, and men, miserably wet and cold, were huddled into rocky crevices and slush-filled foxholes under pitifully thin, canvas shelter-halves. The packed military audience, men from many nations with their WAVES, WAACS, nurses and Red Cross girls, were enjoying the performance. Who were all these people? How could they sit, unmindful and unconcerned, only a few miles removed from all that suffering and destruction? Emotion came close to the surface. Bucky, restless, felt it too. There were angry tears in his eyes. With no words we got up and left before the revue was half through. But once on the outside, on the familiar hard seats of the Jeep, the feeling passed.

We spent the next day with Bill Mauldin and Don Robinson, the talented GIs who wrote and published the 45th Division News, and a very busy last day shopping the black market and supply depots, and visiting men we had evacuated to hospitals. Bucky's sincere and innocent face made him a great scrounger. When the time came to leave, the Jeep was overloaded with everything imaginable (even a side of beef) obtained with phony requisitions or stolen from every supply unit in the area.

We returned in the evening in rain and darkness, but our spirits had revived. We were happy to be going back. At one of the MP checkpoints, a soaked peasant woman with crying baby in arms stood in the muddy road beside us. Bucky looked away uncomfortably for a moment then, with compulsive suddenness, peeled off his newly acquired hooded trench coat and handed it to her as we drove off.

On the 24th, we headed back up the mountain trail. The 1st Battalion section had left a small tree on the altar of the little church. Somehow it seemed like the only place to spend a Christmas Day.

Christmas Day services, Venafro, Italy, 1943

January 1944: Hill # 1083
Originally published January 1964

IN LINE WITH the anniversary theme of this issue and previous reminiscences about World War II, we recall celebrating a cold New Year's Day 20 years ago on mountaintop #1083 high in the Apennines above the town of Venafro, about 30 kilometers east and north of Cassino.

Handicapped by weather, terrain and German defenses, we had inched our way upward to this pinnacle in laborious fashion and had covered a miserly distance of about two miles in all over the two months immediately preceding. The weather during that time had been constantly cold and wet, and not at all like the sunny Italy advertised by the Mediterranean cruise folders. The mountains were rugged and rocky, and the paths and trails were so uniformly narrow that all movement or progress was necessarily made on foot. The Germans retreated grudgingly and by plan, always to higher ranges and peaks from which we were ever under direct observation and effectively immobilized by their artillery fire. Supplies and equipment had to be hauled in by pack board on our own aching backs or by our reluctant mules. The wounded and sick could only be evacuated by litter relay teams down the dangerous foot paths in an eight-to-twelve-hour carry before the nearest Jeep or ambulance could be reached.

Venafro, Italy

The snows began shortly before Christmas, and on New Year's Day we were isolated atop the barren #1083 in a small, stone farmhouse that looked northward across a bleak, white panorama to higher, snow-covered peaks ahead. For the first time, however, in the two uncomfortable months that had climaxed the 114 days of continuous combat since Salerno, our spirits were high, and the New Year held promise of better days ahead. The rumor had been confirmed that we were to be relieved shortly by the French 3rd Algerian Division.

The New Year had been ushered in just at midnight by every gun and artillery piece on each side of the lines, and from our vantage point it was a spectacular show. After the demonstration, as if by mutual agreement, hostilities ceased and there was quiet for the rest of the day. We had a roaring fire going in the farmhouse fireplace, and two of our enterprising scroungers in the aid section had discovered and subdued four young pigs that the *paisanos* and previous occupants had failed to evacuate. During the prolonged and ceremonial cooking, we combined all of our aid-station supply of grain alcohol with an equal amount of lemon drink prepared from the powdered packages in K-rations and served continuous hot grog in canteen cups. It was a memorable and drunken feast. The roast pork and hog jowls were a gourmand's delight. The only thing missing was black eyed peas.

Winter 1944: Come to the Ball
Originally published February 1969

WAR IS ONLY occasionally the gruesome ordeal of blood and battle described dramatically in news accounts (or now pictured so vividly by television-camera reporting). In any full-scale action the number of men who participate in actual front-line combat is comparatively small. On a given day of fighting, unless some unusual situation develops, about one-tenth of a division's troops are engaging the enemy. Although they may be located in the combat zone, the hundreds of supporting units backing up a division are seldom in any significant danger, and the thousands of troops that fill the rear echelons of a theater of operations rarely experience combat except through second-hand rumor.

Volturno valley from mountain location near Venafro

To the individual soldier, front-line duty is more often a scattering of brief-but-memorable experiences—some dangerous, some not—punctuating long periods of inactivity. During the brief encounters, if he is unlucky or foolhardy, he may get captured, wounded or killed, although the percentages against such happenings are much in his favor. During the more frequent intervals of quiet, his chief interests center around feeding his stomach, combating the elements, making himself comfortable, fighting boredom, thinking of women and struggling with his own personality problems. Most commonly he maintains a fairly sound outlook and, with his sense of humor intact, takes advantage of all opportunities to goof off or engage in some of the incongruous, lighthearted undertakings dreamed up by lonely men away from home. This frivolous side of war gets little emphasis, particularly from the dour, pacifist-minded who concentrates on and finds satisfaction in its horrors.

On January 10, 1944, after the 3rd Algerian Regiment of the Free French took over our positions in the snowy mountains above and east of Cassino, we slogged wearily but happily down the mountain trails, wanting nothing more than rest and a change of scenery. We had been on the line for a prolonged stretch of 70 days, although, except for the miserable weather, this was not as bad as it sounds. Nevertheless, we were tired, and the promise of a few weeks of rest and recuperation sounded good to us. No one then would have dreamed that one week later we would be preparing feverishly for a most stupendously staged dinner dance, the Prima Inaugural Overseas Combat Ball, to be held in a sumptuous ballroom of an Italian nobleman's villa.

Our morale got a big boost when we learned that the rest area assigned to us was the familiar locale of Piedimonte d'Alife and San Potito. We had liberated the towns earlier from the hated *Tedeschi* and had made many friends there during our previous relief in October. It was a real homecoming, and the still grateful and still unspoiled townspeople were happy to have us back.

The weather cooperated. The cold was not severe, the rain fell infrequently and the sun warmed the days with the promise of an early spring. Some training exercises and maneuvers were going on, but, in the main, they were minimal and chiefly for the benefit of new replacements. Regulations were winked at, and the policy toward passes was liberal. The men were free to wander off almost without restriction to seek out entertainment and the few *signorinas* not already locked away by their families. Even with the supply limited, they apparently found some (or at least a durable few) because business at the Pro station was constant and good.

There were a number of talented entertainers in the battalion. In the evenings we usually gathered around an open campfire near the kitchen tent to watch the "Baron," one of the riflemen and a former vaudeville magician, run through his professional repertoire of tricks. Pfc. Anastasio Vas, a diminutive Puerto Rican who doubled as a runner for Battalion Headquarters when the kitchen wasn't set up, collected instruments and musicians and held a nightly jam session that ended only when the *vino* ran out, or when the sleepy men in the tent area began throwing shoes. As a civilian, Vas had played the drums for Xavier Cugat, and with a couple of sticks and the kitchen pots and pans to beat on, he filled the nights with frantic Latin rhythms.

It must have been the wild, rhumba beat that catapulted us into the project of staging a dance. Other units were holding banquets and drinking parties, but none had ever conceived an undertaking so ambitious. It was to be an exclusive blowout, just for the 2nd Battalion—but a democratic free-for-all with no officer/enlisted man distinctions. Vas and his crew of musicians were enthusiastic. All five of the kitchen units would furnish the food; F Company agreed to take on rotating sentry duty to make sure that men from other units would not crash the party; G Company would find tables and chairs and build a bandstand; E Company would be in charge of decorations; and H Company already had details out scouting the countryside wine cellars and bargaining for hoarded bottles. All we needed was a time, a place, women and hard liquor.

We chose the evening of January 27 as the time, but in our rural isolation the other requisites presented problems. The Medical Section volunteered to solve them, and we tackled our impossible assignment with optimistic abandon. At the insistence of our young friend, Severino, we called on the Count Gaetano Filangheri, an aging nobleman whose villa a short way down the road toward Gioia had escaped war damage. The villa was in almost as decayed a state as the Count himself, but it did possess a magnificent grand ballroom that opened out onto spacious terraces. It was just what we needed. The Count showed us around personally, and although he trembled slightly and his eyes misted on looking at the hanging crystal chandeliers and marble statuary, he seemed very gracious and hospitable. According to Severino's excited interpreting, the *Conte* was actually overwhelmed with joy, anticipating the honor, and very eager to please his great benefactors, the *Americanos*. We took his consent for granted and left four cartons of cigarettes and two cases of the new 10-in-1 rations as a token of appreciation.

In the next few days we located and visited four field hospitals within a 15-mile radius of Piedimonte. We plastered the bulletin boards of the nurses' quarters with homemade posters announcing and ballyhooing the unparalleled Prima Inaugural Overseas Combat Ball (courtesy, 2nd Battalion, 157th Infantry). We conferred with Chief Nurses and promised anything. Within a short time we had signed up 63 willing Florence Nightingales who couldn't wait to mingle with genuine combat soldiers. On our visits to the hospitals— by requisition, bribery and outright theft—we also accumulated 15 5-gallon tins of absolute (medical) alcohol that would launch the affair in the proper direction. The Battalion Motor Pool would supply 2-ton trucks to transport the nurses to and from the party. Everything fell into place perfectly.

On January 22, the 3rd Division and the British 1st Division landed at Anzio, on the coast 40 miles southwest of Rome. The bold and unexpected sea-borne attack caught the Germans by surprise, and the invading forces met almost no resistance. However, the Allies exploited their advantage too cautiously; this gave the Germans time to react, and within a few days, they were pouring in massive numbers of troops to ring the beachhead. It was obvious that additional support would be called for.

As the only veteran major unit with amphibious training not then in action, the 45th Division was a logical choice. Without even a preliminary alert, the orders returning us to action came through from Fifth Army Headquarters in Caserta on the afternoon of January 25. We had 12 hours to pack up and move out.

There were no opportunities to cancel our plans and obligations; there was no time for goodbyes. It was barely dawn when our convoy rolled by Count Filangheri's villa on our way to the staging area at Pozzuoli above Naples. On the afternoon of January 28 the Navy landed us on the beaches at Anzio.

Cynics maintained that the wily old Count, through connections in Caserta at the King's Palace in which Mark Clark had set up Fifth Army Headquarters, knew of the Anzio plans from the start, knew our departure date before we did and was certain all along that a dance would never take place. We have always preferred to feel, however, that as the illustrious and honored host for the spectacular Prima Inaugural Overseas Combat Ball, the *Conte* must have suffered a great disappointment.

Spring 1944: La Signora de Benedetti
Originally published March 1977

L AST OCTOBER ON a visit to Italy, we renewed acquaintance with Signora Luciana de Benedetti-Arditi. We had first met this attractive lady on July 4, 1975, at a luncheon for General Mark Clark given by the mayors of Anzio and Nettuno, whose twin cities on the Tyrrhenian coast some 40 miles southwest of Rome were the scene of so much devastation during the World War II spring of 1944.

At that luncheon, she had sat quietly at the head table, taking in all the flowery talk as the mayors complimented General Clark and listening intently to the general's version of his battle for the Anzio beachhead 31 years before. It was evident then, that the Signora could have added a few words of her own to the story, but the formalities were such that she politely held her tongue and smiled sweetly through it all.

This past year we had lunch with her again at one of the sidewalk tables in Rome's Piazza Navona, and a week later, visited with her in Anzio for afternoon tea at her farm home near the Ospedale Civile, and just behind the grounds and villa of her old friend, Prince Stefano Borghese. She told us her story of Anzio, and it was most interesting. She thought the Americans and British were pretty stupid not to have gone on to Rome when they had the chance.

Signora de Benedetti is a sprightly widow in her early seventies: a tiny wisp of a woman with twinkling eyes, a bubbly sense of humor and an excellent command of English. Although she maintains a small apartment in Rome on the Via Aurelia Antica west of the Tiber, she prefers to spend most of her time on her farm at Anzio. She lives alone in the remodeled barn and cattle-shed there (the family villa was, destroyed during the fighting 33 years ago), and her farm vineyard raises grapes, which she sells to the local cooperative; but her main energies are devoted to the lawn and flower gardens, which surround her home. She drives an ancient British Morris, and a trip with her through the crowded streets of downtown Rome is an eye-opening experience. ("I drive—how do you say it in English—jerky?")

Her husband, who was a nationally known Italian sculptor, died several years ago. Her children are grown and live away—a son close by in Rome and two daughters in Northern Italy. But all of the family were together at Anzio during the war years and remained there throughout all of the unbelievable destruction that accompanied the almost five months, of bitter, continuous struggle for that small bit of beach frontage. She remembers those days with some amusement now.

After Italy capitulated in September 1943 and the Germans took over the country and put it under military occupation, the de Benedettis were forced out of their farm villa by the commanding colonel of a German unit stationed there. "He was a very ugly, nasty man," she recalled. "I pretended I didn't understand German, and for several weeks I refused to move. But finally when his general came and threatened to pack all of us off to a labor camp, I had to give in."

Later, the "ugly" colonel was transferred, and a younger, more pleasant German officer took over. "This one was very nice, with kind eyes. He was a gentleman and very polite, and the reason he wanted my house was because of my grand piano. He played very well."

In early January 1944, about two weeks before the Allies landed at Anzio, the gentlemanly German officer took her aside and confided that he and his unit were being moved up the coast to Civitavecchia, about 50 miles north of Rome, where they were expecting an invasion by sea.

"He told us that we could move back into the villa and that all of the German troops were leaving the area.

"We were living in the villa again when the Americans and British came. One night this terrible noise and rumbling woke us up. We didn't know what was going on, and we stayed awake until dawn. Then this young American lieutenant burst through the door and pointed his carbine at us. I said, 'Don't shoot! Don't shoot! I speak English!' I told him all the Germans were gone and that he should drive straight on into Rome. Later I told the American and British officers the same thing."

The Allies failed to take advantage of the initial surprise of the Anzio landings and proceeded much too cautiously. The Germans had time to move troops back in from all over Italy and surround the beachhead. Many weeks later, when the fighting was at its peak, an ammunition dump, which had been established on the de Benedetti farm, was bombed and their villa was completely destroyed. The family escaped miraculously and moved into the Borghese villa with their neighbors, the Prince and his sister.

In April the Fifth Army moved advance headquarters up to Anzio and into the Borghese villa and grounds. "They were very nice to us," said Signora de Benedetti. "My husband was permitted to live upstairs with the officers, but the children and I had to move down into the cellar with the enlisted men. The GIs were very kind. They dug a foxhole big enough for all three children, and we kept them in it for the next two months. I used to sneak up at night to see my husband, but we could never get much sleep because of the terrible shelling and bombing. But, of course, we were much younger then, and we didn't mind it too much."

It was almost dark as we finished tea on the small, covered terrace of the de Benedetti farmhouse. The Signora urged us to finish the cake she had made. "Do you remember that lunch last year with General Clark?" she asked. "I listened to him tell about all the planning and about how clever they were to capture Rome. I wanted to get up and tell about all the Germans being gone and how they could have gotten there five months sooner if they had just listened to me—but then, I didn't want to spoil his story."

Sloppy George
Originally published February 1974

THE ODDS FINALLY caught up with George when a German machine-gunner did him in. It happened at Anzio, 30 years ago in February 1944. I can't remember the exact time of it now, but it may have been on the same day that our group was captured while trying to evacuate a bunch of wounded through the German lines. Actually, I didn't hear about it until four months later when a couple of 2nd Battalion men, picked up later in the Italian campaign, turned up at our POW camp in Poland.

George was sloppy. He didn't make an impressive-looking soldier. His uniform never fit; his permanently wrinkled shirt hung loosely from sloping shoulders and bunched at the wrists; his trousers, always dirty, half in and half out of erratically laced leggings, bagged in all the wrong places. His clumsy GI shoes stayed scuffed and dusty. Except for an unkempt thatch of pale straw hair poking out over owlish eyes that peered through steel-rimmed spectacles, his head practically disappeared within his combat helmet.

It probably never occurred to him, but George had to be the most educated and intellectual soldier in the Regiment. He had gone to Phillips Exeter, graduated summa cum laude from Harvard and had just finished law school there when he volunteered for basic training. Whether he had considered (or could have been considered for) officer candidate school was doubtful.

At any rate, George seemed happy as an enlisted man and, for two years, served uncomplainingly as the intelligence corporal in our Battalion S2 section. He was methodical and diligent in his work, and there was never a hint of disdain, superiority or antagonism in his relation or attitude toward any of the officers who headed his section from time to time. He was pleasant and even-tempered, and his quiet, philosophical manner made him seem almost shy. His good mind and his great language fluency in German made him invaluable to the battalion; his thorough and unemotional interrogation of prisoners produced results. He never shirked an assignment, and on patrol and reconnaissance missions, he appeared oblivious to danger and, on occasion, even reckless.

Although he was always friendly and often humorous, it was extremely difficult to draw him out in conversation. The only man in the Regiment who really got to know George was his last boss, Jack Weiner, the officer in charge of our Battalion Intelligence. Weiner, a product of Chicago's Southside and a University of Michigan football scholarship, was dark, heavyset, handsome, energetic, loud and extrovertish—a constant comic with an unending store of Yiddish jokes. It always tickled George that Weiner was married to a redheaded, Irish nurse from Murphy, North Carolina. In the months of combat through Sicily and Italy, a deep bond of affection had developed between them.

When the battalion earned its Presidential Unit Citation during the Battle of the Caves on the Anzio beachhead, George stuck to his work and did an outstanding job. There were only two hundred survivors of that ten-day ordeal, and the stories of individual heroism were so plentiful it wasn't unusual that the one about George cut down by a burst of machine gun fire while trying to rescue Weiner, got overlooked and quickly forgotten.

But there must have been a touch of irony and a twinge of bitterness when the official notice of his having been killed in action was delivered to his family in the States. Especially to his father, George Sylvester Viereck, Sr., the famous anti-communist, pro-German intellectual, spending the war in the federal penitentiary at Atlanta, where he had been jailed for years as a suspected Nazi sympathizer.

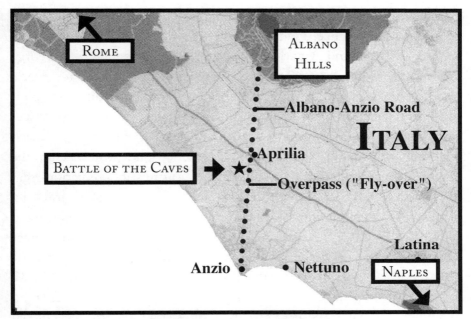

Anzio–Nettuno – Battle of the Caves
January – February 1944

Anzio, 1944
Originally published March 1969

IN THE OVERALL picture of European strategy during World War II, the campaign at Anzio was of negligible importance, yet for months it dominated news reports. With Russia impatiently calling for a second front, and the Allied advance in Italy stalled at the Cassino-Venafro line, the Anzio landing was carried out at the insistence of Winston Churchill. It had two main purposes: to break the deadlock on the winter line to the south, and to capture Rome for propaganda purposes.

The initial landing achieved complete surprise and met almost no German resistance. Had the American commander in charge of the joint British and American operation been someone like George Patton, the objectives might have been accomplished within a week. Instead the Allies proceeded too cautiously and, by failing to exploit their initial advantage, allowed the Germans to mobilize forces from as far away as Southern France and Yugoslavia. The beachhead was soon ringed by massive numbers of men and armor. After the easy and successful landing, Churchill's optimistic prediction that Rome would be liberated within a few days, only served to infuriate Hitler to a point of frenzy. The Führer became equally determined to lance "this abscess south of Rome," annihilate the invading forces and sweep them into the sea. The narrow strip of coastline became the scene of the most bitter and prolonged battle of World War II.

The Navy landed us on the beaches north of Anzio on the afternoon of January 28, six days after the initial invasion, and the beachhead was still quiet. The weather was chilly but pleasant, and the sun was shining. The gently rolling, fertile, reclaimed farmlands stretched inland for 15 or 20 miles where, in the distance, the Alban Hills rising to three thousand feet were obscured in a purple gray haze. Crops were growing, and the forests of pine and cork in the Padiglione Woods where we first bivouacked were fresh and green. The sea, beneath the colorful sunset to our west, was smooth and peaceful. There was nothing forbidding about any of it, and after the cold and rain and snow of the mountains, it seemed like a Garden of Eden.

Colonel Brown, our brand new Battalion Commander, had joined us in the staging area at Pozzuoli, north of Naples, just before sailing. He was young, "Regular Army," fresh from the States, and had never been in combat before. His inexperience and his personality conflicts with some of his staff officers soon set off a chain of events that turned us all into reluctant heroes and eventually denied Hitler the satisfaction of another Dunkirk.

Although the battle at Anzio continued for more than four months and Rome was not liberated until the first week in June, the intense fighting took place between February 3 and March 2, and the fate of the beachhead was decided by a convulsive struggle of epic proportion in the five days between February 16–20. By the first days of February, the Germans had more than 10 divisions of infantry and armor ready and planned to attack in three phases. We all stayed busy digging in, rolling barbed wire, setting up fields of fire and laying mine fields. It was a new experience for the 45th Division; we had never fought a defensive battle before.

Troops digging Allied defenses at Anzio

The first two savage attacks came on February 3–5 and February 7–10 and were directed down the axis of the main road that led from Rome and Albano to the port at Anzio. We were involved in both of them, but the British just to our right and straddling the road took the heaviest punishment. By the end of the second phase, the Germans had succeeded in driving the British out of the strategic "Factory" town of Aprilia and wiping out the salient projecting north along the road that had denied them an approach for their heavy armor. The stubborn British brigades were intact but reduced to half-strength and badly battered.

Just before midnight on February 14 our 2nd Battalion advanced along the Albano road to take over the positions of the bone-weary remnants of the Irish Guard Brigade. As we moved forward in the quiet darkness, the only sounds to be heard were the constant low rumble of motor convoys and the clank of tank treads in the distance ahead of us. The atmosphere was one of ominous suspense, and not at all reassuring. We had turned off the road to the left and were being guided by one of the jittery Irish guards when the silence exploded suddenly into rattling machine guns, rifle fire and the unholy screams and bursts of six-barreled mortars, and the whole countryside lighted up in the eerie green glare of soaring Very lights overhead. The open rolling land all around us was an unearthly scene of devastation, twisted wire, wrecked equipment, half-dug foxholes and unburied dead. Panic gripped all of us as we froze to the ground trying to find protection where there was none. For what seemed like hours, we advanced in brief, breathless spurts during the intervals of semi-darkness between flares, shell bursts and red, zipping tracers overhead. We finally reached a thicket-filled ravine and followed it. When our guide led us into a cave opening that led underground to other passages where we found the Battalion Headquarters already set up, the feeling of relief was almost overwhelming.

The Caves of Pozzolana, scene of heavy fighting during
Battle of the Caves, February 1944

The Caves of Pozzolana, excavated for building material and used more recently by sheepherders, were a fantastic maze of underground, crisscrossing passages dug into a ridge of shale and sandstone and opening onto the exterior gullies and knolls in 15 or 20 places. The command posts of Battalion Headquarters, G and H Companies, were located in passages near some of the cave entrances, separated in places by corridors one-hundred-or-more yards long. Crowded into one of the larger passages were 60 or 70 terrified peasants, mostly old men, women and children, who had found shelter there in the days before as the battle lines raged back and forth over their homes and lands.

The day of February 15 was relatively quiet. We set up our medical aid station in the corridor behind the headquarters group. Our Jeep and trailer, which had tried to follow us up into position the night before, had been hit and lay useless about 150 yards out from one of the cave openings on exposed ground. Somehow during the night of the 15th, we managed to get out to it and salvaged about three-fourths of the medical supplies. In the hours before dawn on the 16th, the entire beachhead grew quiet, as if both sides were holding their breath, ticking off the minutes. And then it started.

Every artillery piece on the beachhead opened up at one time, our naval guns joined in, and for the next 45 minutes the steady thunder of guns and exploding shells rolled on. The front lines disappeared under dense clouds of drifting smoke and dust. The Germans launched attacks in dozens of places along the entire perimeter, but all were diversionary except for the main thrust (four miles across) down the Albano-Anzio road where they planned to break through and split the beachhead in half. Massed troops poured over the open ground, wave after wave with tanks in support. They fell by the hundreds and the slaughter was terrific. But they kept coming, hour after hour, day after day.

By the night of the 18th, after two and one-half days of continuous battle, we had treated over 200 wounded and we had collected 120 litter cases in the aid-station corridor. No one had slept. We were out of plasma, morphine and bandages, and almost out of food. We had to recruit some of the peasant women to help nurse the wounded and set others to work cooking soup out of the few chickens and dried beans they had brought with them into the caves. Later in the night, Stan Lemon, our Regimental Demolitions Officer, got up to us with some borrowed tanks and half-tracks of the 6th Armored and brought in supplies; he was able to evacuate all of the litter wounded. Meanwhile, on our right flank across the road, the lines had been driven back almost two miles; on our left, a mile.

We sat in on most of the headquarters conferences. Colonel Brown, a little dazed by this kind of baptism after so short a time in command, was more than a little unsure of himself. Captain George Kessler, our veteran and capable Executive Officer, bore the burden of the strain. He organized defenses, shifted remnants of this platoon here, moved a heavy weapons squad there, pulled in isolated outposts and drove himself day and night without rest. As the fighting grew in intensity, Brown withdrew further into his shell. His plans and orders were often conflicting and confusing, and it was Kessler who translated and altered them into some semblance of workability. Upset by our growing casualties, our difficulties with supply and our impossible position, Kessler and the rest of us argued for withdrawal. Brown, feeling his own inexperience and annoyed by his increasing dependence on Kessler, reacted by becoming more autocratic, more suspicious of our motives and more obstinate in his determination to hold the positions. None of us relished the thought of moving back through the open hell going on outside, and, like most of us, Brown may have been afraid to leave the comparative shelter of the caves.

On the night of the 19th, we were again able to evacuate another 50 litter cases. Again there was an opportunity to withdraw; but, again, Brown could not be budged. Kessler, torn between his compassion for the troops and his reluctant duty toward Brown, never lost his composure and deployed the ever shrinking strength of the battalion in a manner that kept it effective as a point of resistance. By morning we were completely cut off, and the remnants of the battalion were entirely confined to the caves. Brown issued orders; Kessler ignored them and juggled the weary men as best he could. There was no possibility of escape now, and we had to make the best of the situation.

We didn't know that when the Germans failed to break through the final defenses two miles to our rear on the 19th, their all-out offensive had finally cracked. The fighting continued unabated, but there were no more waves of reserves to be thrown into the attack, and the exhausted German troops had reached the limit of their endurance. An Allied counterattack on the 20th threw them into more confusion, and, on the evening of the 21st, the 2nd Battalion of the Queen's Royal Regiment fought their way through the mixed-up lines in an attempt to rescue us and reinforce the cave positions. Unfortunately, they had bumped into strong German forces on the way, and, when they reached us, they had lost most of their supplies, ammunition and supporting weapons. The relief force now needed relief.

Our predicament in the caves was still critical. There were German forces all around us, and they were still trying to dislodge us by storming the cave openings. Men were fighting hand to hand with knives, bayonets and rifle butts. To keep the Germans out, we had to call on our own artillery to blast the cave entrances. The din within the corridors was terrific, and the concussion waves left most of us with shattered eardrums.

The British talked Colonel Brown into withdrawing, and on the night of the 22nd, what remained of the 2nd Battalion left the caves in small groups to try and make their way back. Since we had another 30 litter cases still in the caves, six of us from the medical section stayed on with the British, hoping that if anyone got back, some scheme of evacuation could be worked out. The British, meanwhile, decided that their own position in the caves was untenable. They planned to fight their way out shortly after nightfall on the 23rd and called for an artillery barrage to begin at dusk and cover their retreat.

Late in the afternoon, Hugo Fielschmidt, the 157th's zany Regimental Dental Officer, stumbled flushed and wild-eyed into the caves. Under the impression that a temporary truce would be in effect so that both sides could clear the area of wounded, he had volunteered to lead a group of litter bearers through more than a mile of German-held territory. They had come on foot with Hugo waving a Red Cross flag. Once on the way up, when some shelling had started, he was forced to jump into the nearest foxhole on top of two astonished Germans. They were more astonished when he scrambled out after the shelling and went blithely on his way waving the flag.

With rescue seemingly near, we did not stop to weigh our chances or consider the difficulties that lay before us. There was no time to lose because of the British escape plan. We loaded the wounded onto litters and had to scratch around among the British, the walking wounded and the stragglers to find enough manpower to assign one bearer to each end of a litter. With Fielschmidt still waving his red and white flag, we led the column out of the caves. After 10 days of underground darkness, the late afternoon daylight was almost blinding. Most of the litter bearers, all utterly exhausted from the sleepless days and nights of battle were unable to carry their loads more than a few yards at a time without stopping to rest. After the constant cold of the caves, the warm, oppressively humid air sapped our remaining energies. The column proceeded slowly. The whole area through which we struggled was an incredible panorama of desolation and destruction—wrecked vehicles and armor, up-rooted trees and blasted vegetation, discarded ammunition and equipment, not one foot of ground unmarked by shell craters and, lying everywhere, the dead.

We were a strange-looking procession, and we passed within arm's reach of many groups of German soldiers busily digging in. But they only seemed curious and did not molest us. We had covered about half the distance when we passed a crumbled farmhouse concealing a German tank. A German major and staff sergeant stepped out from behind the house and halted us. The major indicated we could go no farther.

There followed an unbelievable, comic opera interlude of argument through interpreters. We maintained that we should be allowed to proceed; the major held that we must be taken to German headquarters. Fielschmidt, red-faced and angry, his arms flailing wildly, shouted that this was a hell of a way to honor a truce; we were noncombatants, and, according to the Geneva Convention, couldn't be captured. He threatened the German major with court martial!

The argument seemed to go on forever, but the Germans were adamant. Time was growing short; dusk was almost on us, and with it the barrage called for by the British would soon roll over where we were standing. We quieted Fielschmidt and reluctantly agreed to be captured. The ridiculousness of the whole episode—a debate on the ethics of warfare on a stage setting of carnage and destruction—struck us and the German major simultaneously. We laughed and bowed politely.

The column was turned around, and, now accompanied by armed guards, we headed to the left toward the Albano road to join the German Army. When we reached the next rise, we looked back. The German major was doubled over and still visibly shaking with laughter.

***

From the book, *Anzio: the Massacre at the Beachhead*, by British author and former war correspondent, Wynford Vaughan-Thomas:

> But the battalion had a commander, Lt. Col. Laurence C. Brown, who refused to allow himself to be dismayed. He turned the caves into a fortress, ignoring the fact that he was completely cut off from his base. . . . He was destined to fight a private war for more than six days—and to hold the western shoulder at all costs.
>
> Out of the 900 men at the beginning of the week's fighting, the 2nd Battalion 157th Regiment succeeded in mustering only 200 after their retreat from the caves. Out of this remnant more than 100 were battle casualties. They had held the western flank of the salient

against enormous odds and fought one of the most memorable infantry battles in the annals of the American Army. . . . They looked more like scarecrows than soldiers, but they had earned with their battered bodies the rare honour of a Presidential Unit Citation.

We have often wondered whether Brown and the rest of us should qualify as heroes or just as ordinary cowards trapped by circumstance, too frightened to run.

Reminiscing, World War II
Originally published December 1974

THIRTY-ONE YEARS AGO in December 1943, the fighting on the Cassino front in Italy was building in intensity. The British 56th (Black Cat) Division, a battle-weary, veteran unit of the long Africa Campaign and continuously in action since the Salerno Beachhead, had successfully secured Mt. Camino and was moving onward toward the Garigliano River, which had to be crossed before Cassino itself could come under direct attack. After another two months of bitter fighting there under the most miserable weather conditions and with the Cassino line still unbreached, the 56th was pulled out without any significant period of rest and was shuttled up by sea to the beleaguered Anzio beachhead south of Rome. The Division reached there just as the Allied forces, already reeling after the first German attacks, were making frantic preparations to withstand the major German effort that was soon to follow.

We met Maurice Harvey for the first time on the evening of February 21, 1944, when his 2/7th Battalion of the Queen's Royal Regiment (West Surrey), 56th Division, fought its way up to the Anzio caves where the remnants of our own battered battalion, after 10 days of mortal combat behind the German lines, still struggled to survive.

The valiant effort was not overly successful, as the Queen's lost all of its equipment and more than half of its men in attempting to rescue us.

Two days later, Dr. Harvey and I found ourselves uncomfortably quartered in an eight-by-ten-foot earthen bunker dug into the bank of a dry stream bed, helping grizzled-but-kindly Feldwebel Herbert Mihler from Chemnitz-am-Sachsen run the medical aid station for the Wehrmacht's 1027 Panzer Grenadiers. We were kept there for two weeks, finally traveling together next to the temporary prison cages at Rome's Cinema City, and then onward by truck and boxcar through Bolzano and the Brenner Pass to the prison camp at Moosburg, close by Munich. We parted company in May 1944 when the American officer prisoners in Moosburg were shipped north to Poland.

Two months ago, *The Bulletin* printed a poem by Dr. Harvey, along with some of his observations about the National Health Service in Britain. Recently he sent us another contribution—this time a nostalgic, wartime reminiscence about those miserable but somehow wondrous and inspiring days of combat in the war-torn Italy of December 1943.

Gift of the Gods by M.W. Harvey

During the rough and tumble years of the War, one made many acquaintances, and even a few real friends, only to lose touch with them, as often as not, suddenly, and with startling finality.

It was in Italy in December 1943—not the sunny Italy of romantic fancy, but the Italy where the more fortunate armies of the ancients used to go into winter quarters. An Italy of rain and sleet and even quite a lot of snow, especially on the high ground. An Italy that was not at all a pleasant place for a winter campaign, especially sleeping in the open, as one was forced to do on occasion. It was in this real Italy of December 1943 that I was posted to an infantry battalion, which had its headquarters in a village where life was reasonably safe, provided that one was careful. That is to say, provided one ran as fast as possible across certain places where gaps between houses left one in full view of the Germans not far away on the other side of the river. For reasons best known to himself, Jerry did not often shell the place at that time.

As I have said, the weather was vile; but we were fairly comfortable and had the place almost entirely to ourselves, most of the inhabitants having taken themselves elsewhere, very sensibly.

Among my fellow sufferers of all ranks, there were many whom I remember well, though seldom by name. There was the C.O. Some said he was too reckless to be a good unit commander, and perhaps they were right; but he was far less careless of the safety of those under his command than of his own. He was the only man whom I have ever had the chance to observe closely and yet remain in doubt whether he really knew fear. Perhaps he was a convinced fatalist, perhaps merely supremely unimaginative. Some called him "Stunter"—behind his back—and said that he was an exhibitionist. But if he was acting a part, he acted it superbly. He never seemed to take the most elementary precautions for his own safety, yet he came through the whole war without a scratch. I could not help wondering what would have happened had he been wounded, however slightly.

Then there was another officer whose name I forget, so I will call him simply "the Major." The title is apt to conjure up the vision of an elderly, red-faced warrior, a bottle- (repeat), bottle-scarred veteran with a white moustache whose dreary reminiscences are the despair of unwilling audiences in saloon bars and similar places. But the Major in question wasn't like that. Everyone liked him. He was in his early twenties, efficient and conscientious without being officious. And he was able to keep the friendship of older men with longer service, even after being promoted over their heads. I can imagine few better testimonials.

Soon after I joined the unit, we were sent to cross the river. It was a nasty little river, very cold and muddy looking, that ran westward through a broad valley between high hills. The hills looked very pretty no doubt in their snowy mantles, but it was difficult to wax enthusiastic when we had to spend hours on end on our bellies in the mud or in a wet slit trench. In the valley there was no snow, but plenty of cold, sticky mud, not quite so bad as that of Tunisia, but bad enough.

According to the precedent, Division had made elaborate plans that were marred by Division's own failure to take into account various simple, easily ascertained facts. The result of this oversight was that things did not go according to plan, but only according to precedent. However, our battalion did get across, somewhat the worse for the experience and a good 12 hours late. But nobody else got across at all, apart from a few Polish commandos sent with us to cut telephone lines and throats behind the German lines. We saw few of them again, and were left marooned on the north side of the river, surrounded by very irritated Germans and on the wrong side of an almost equally angry little river. No doubt the Poles had annoyed the Germans, but we had done nothing to the river except to cross it.

However, the position was not too bad. Most of us were on the reverse slope of the hills just out of reach of the presents that Jerry kept lobbing over to us. My R.A.P. was in a school, solidly built of stone and facing downhill away from the enemy. It is true that the top had been blown off and the back rooms were full of debris, but the big classroom in front was intact and watertight. The only snag was that we had to keep the door shut and the windows shuttered to keep out flying fragments from the shells always exploding a little lower down on the hillside.

On one occasion, having been called out to treat a casualty and doing what I could, I was doubling back to the R.A.P. and, on rounding the corner, saw the Colonel sitting comfortably on a stone beside the path. He was not even wearing a steel helmet, but had his service cap comfortably on the back of his head and a cigarette in his mouth. He was contemplating the shelling with apparent interest. Doubtless to a disembodied spirit it would have proved fascinating, but I did not feel inclined to linger and enjoy it. However, he called to me as I came past and began to chat quite calmly on matters of no importance. Personally, I wished him in a warmer climate than that of Southern Italy in winter, but it is not easy to argue with the C.O. of the unit to which one is attached. I did venture to remark that, for medical reasons at least, the wearing of tin hats was the fashion locally, but the hint was beneath his notice. So there we remained for some minutes, talking of supremely unimportant matters, and watching shell after shell land on a broad muddy patch near a spring at the foot of the hill.

I observed how the fragments from each shell would tear up the turf and the peculiar pattern formed in every case. Most of the fragments flew forward in the general direction of the shell's flight, very few more than about thirty degrees on either side, and fewer yet backwards. This observation proved important, for presently one shell landed nearer and on hard ground. A considerable amount of earth and pebbles fell all around us, and some of it on us. The Colonel grinned cheerfully and remarked that it was getting a trifle warm, so perhaps we had better move. I agreed heartily, and we parted. I hurried off toward the safety and comfort of the R.A.P. while he strolled off quite happily in the opposite direction. Probably he was whistling. If he was acting a part, he carried it off magnificently. And all for an audience of one—or two, including himself.

But while things were not too bad for the rest of us, the Major and his company were certainly catching it. Theirs was the uncomfortable task of guarding the one, very inadequate river crossing by which we could get supplies. So they had to dig in on the wet, flat ground nearby, exposed to constant, heavy shelling. The Major and his batman had dug an extra-long trench for the two of them, as was often done to reduce the amount of work.

Some while after my chat with the Colonel, a runner summoned the Major to Battalion H.Q. for conference. So off he went, at the double, like any sensible man, and arrived safely at the dilapidated house that served as H.Q. Afterward, he returned to his company, also on the double, to find a large hole where his trench had been.

A shell had landed in it and the unfortunate batman had been blown to pieces. But such tragedies were too frequent to cause more than passing comment, whereas the Major's escape seemed providential.

A few days later we were relieved when another unit got across the river a few miles downstream. We were withdrawn for a brief rest, and then sent back to relieve our rescuers. Things were much quieter now, and there were even a few days of fine sunny weather that seemed almost warm after the rain and sleet of the previous weeks.

On such a day, the Colonel and the Major were walking with two others (I forget why) on the south side of a steep, terraced hill, comfortably out of sight and reach of Jerry. Their route took them from one terrace to another higher up the hill. The Colonel went first, and then the other two. But before the Major could follow, a short, stray shell arrived out of the blue. It was a mere harassing shell, fired at a venture, but, like the arrow that felled King Ahab, it found its mark. The other three were unharmed, but the Major was dead before they could get down to him. I think his death depressed all ranks, for he was generally liked. And yet I have forgotten his name.

This story proves nothing, of course—but that should be a refreshing change in an age of statistics that prove anything, according to how they are cooked.

February 1944: Battle of the Caves
Originally published February 1964

THE MESSAGE FROM Dr. Maurice Harvey, Monmouth, U.K., in the discussion of socialized medicine (*Bulletin*, February 1964) brought back memories of our experiences together on the Anzio beachhead in 1944.

Functioning medically as a lowly Battalion Surgeon with the 2nd Battalion of the 157th Infantry Regiment, we had undergone an interesting 10-day ordeal by combat that saw the battalion strength reduced from nearly a thousand men to a battered and sleepless group of two hundred survivors. Unfortunately for us we were surviving still in our original position, which by then was about two miles on the wrong side of the German front line. Psychologically there were many reasons why the battalion remnant found itself in such an awkward spot, but boiled down, our predicament was due to a new commanding officer who was too inexperienced in combat, too bull-headed for his own (and our) good and too scared to retreat. We were cut-off, isolated, bone-tired and slap-happy.

On the evening of February 22, Captain Maurice Harvey of the Royal Army Medical Corps joined us in the cave positions we occupied. He came as part of the Queen's Regiment of the British Black Cat Division that somehow had fought its way through to rescue us. Unfortunately again, in getting up to us, the Queen's had lost half of its men and almost all of its equipment, which only compounded the predicament by adding their misery to our own. One day later we were captured while attempting a daylight evacuation of wounded through the German positions, and about 12 hours later Harvey was captured when the British tried to fight their way back.

On February 24, along with Captain Harvey and two of our own aid-station men, Sergeant "Red" Watkins and Corporal Louie Caronte, we found ourselves snugly situated in a straw-floored, reinforced bunker dug into the side bank of a dry river bed. The Germans had appropriated our services as "noncombatants" and installed our small group in the aid station of the 1027 Panzer Grenadiers to help take care of casualties. This did not really suit any of us, particularly since the 1027 Panzer Grenadiers were occupying front-line positions and were being plastered daily and nightly by the very impressive Allied artillery and naval gunfire. However, we were not in a position where our arguments seemed to carry much weight, so for the next two weeks we ran their aid station and learned how the other half lived.

In civilian days prior to 1940, "Red" Watkins had been the morgue attendant at the Denver General Hospital; Lou Caronte had worked in the Shirley Temple Doll Factory in East Brooklyn. Watkins was a cheerful, red-faced boozer who suffered loudly about being separated from his regular, daily supply of American grain alcohol. Lou Caronte was a pudgy comic with an infectious good humor and a practical approach to any disaster. The one German medic, Feldwebel Herbert Mihler from Chemnitz-am-Sachsen, who shared the tight quarters with us, was a delightful and impressionable veteran of about 50 who had spent two unhappy years on the Russian front. Whenever Mihler would speak of his experiences there, he would roll his eyes heavenward and mutter, "Ooooo, Doktors. Barbarians! Barbarians!" Watkins and Caronte somehow conned the pleasant Mihler into obtaining extra rations of the daily schnapps, which at least alleviated some of Watkins' withdrawal symptoms and helped our general morale.

For two weeks we led a confined but relatively comfortable life. Any venture away from the protection of the dugout was necessarily brief because of the constant and unmerciful Allied shelling. A trip to the nearby latrine area was always a precarious adventure, and all of us, more than once, had the experience of being caught with our pants down in the middle of a rolling barrage. Harvey was not fond of Germans in any form, and after it became apparent that the all-out German offensive, which had boastfully expected to push the entire Allied beachhead into the sea within a matter of hours, had stalled for good, he took pleasure in needling Mihler and the other Germans who occasionally stopped by to visit. Mihler's often expressed hope that we all would stop fighting each other and join forces to fight the Bolshevik enemy failed to impress any of us.

Harvey sported a disorderly, bush-like mustache that had been growing since he had been pushed off the beach at Dunkirk, and although Maurice detested it, he had vowed never to shave it off until Hitler and Germany were no more. Despite the needling, Mihler was fascinated with Harvey, and he never tired of the daily ritual of nudging us slyly, then banging on his metal canister and shouting, "Essen,

Doktors! Essen!" Whereupon he would double up with laughter as the usually supine and somnolent Harvey would jerk to his feet and, with helmet askew and mess-tin in hand, bolt through the bunker entrance for the chow line.

The equipment in a German aid station was meager and in no way comparable to the profusion of stuff in a similar American set-up. By that time in the war, the German shortage of supply was already evident; bandages were of paper, morphia was scarce and plasma was nonexistent. Aside from the leaden loaves of sour, black bread that apparently stayed edible forever, a currant jam and some cheese, the food ration came from whatever was available in the local area of German occupation; their ersatz coffee looked and tasted like a sawdust brew. The little medical work we were called upon to do was limited to doling out the German version of APC, giving an infrequent shot for pain and bandaging shrapnel wounds. The German troops were disciplined and stoic. If there was anything comparable to the American goof-off and sick-book rider in the German Army, none ever appeared at the 1027 Panzer Grenadier aid station. Maybe that's why they didn't need much equipment.

After two weeks, and through the efforts of an understanding German Catholic Chaplain, we were finally permitted to leave the front lines. As we climbed aboard the supply truck that was to evacuate us to Rome, old Mihler, disconsolate at our departure, assured us that we would get special treatment as prisoners because of our work. He would have been happy to go with us. In a touching scene and with a sentimental tear in his eye, he told us not to worry and sent us off with a nostalgic parting we were to hear repeated many times, *"Alles ist besser in Deutschland."*

Part Three

Prisoner of War

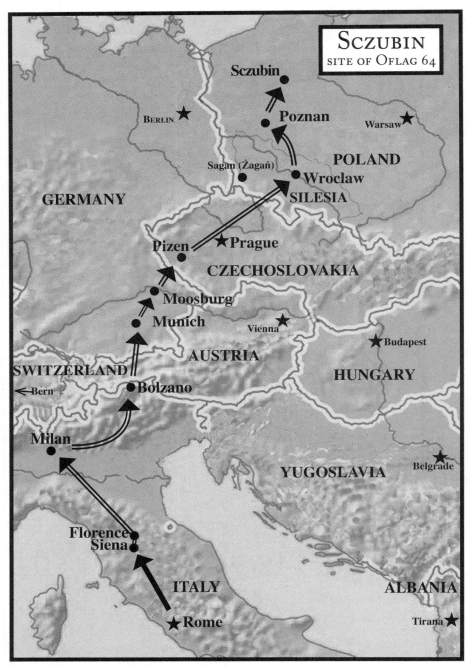

From Rome to Oflag 64 , Sczubin, Poland
By rail (German POW troop transport)
February – May 1944

1944: By Train to Munich
Originally published May 1969

T HE MOST MEMORABLE portion of our first three months as a German war prisoner was the train ride from Italy to Bavaria. Our Pullman was a standard boxcar of the 40 and 8 variety, which we shared with an unusual group of fellow prisoners. In the five days it took us to make what should have been an overnight run, we learned the essentials of communal living in adverse circumstances.

After our capture on the Anzio beachhead in late February, we were detained for two weeks on the front lines where we helped run the medical aid station for a German combat unit (*Bulletin*, February 1964). All during that interesting interval we had been pounded day and night by our own ground and naval artillery. It was a great relief, finally, to say goodbye to the sounds of combat, the 1027 Panzer Grenadiers, and ride their supply truck into Rome.

In Rome we were cooped up for 10 days in one of the sound stages at Cine Citta, where the Germans had established a temporary prisoner-collecting compound. When they had accumulated enough officer-prisoners to make up a load, we were off again by truck to a camp on the outskirts of Siena, about 60 miles away to the north. It was from Siena, two weeks later, that our train journey began.

A few days before leaving Rome, we were joined by the bumptious group of officers who were to be our boxcar companions on the trip through Northern Italy and the Alps. They arrived in a bunch, assured and unintimidated, a mixed bag of individualists. Excepting two young American airmen, they were all British or British Colonials. Most were English, but the group also included two Scotsmen, four Indians, a Welshman, a Canadian, a Rhodesian and a New Zealander. They sported a few odds and ends of battle dress, but for the most part they were clothed in disreputable peasant rags. They had many bonds in common. All had been captured more than a year before, during the African campaign, and all had once been in the same camp at Chianti on the Italian Adriatic. In September 1943, during the brief interval between Italy's capitulation and the German takeover, they had taken advantage of the confusion and escaped into the mountains. There for six months, alone or in groups of two, they had hidden out with friendly peasant families and lived off the countryside. After the Anzio landings, expecting Rome to be liberated momentarily, they had worked their way toward the Eternal City and freedom, only to be picked up by an extensive Fascist drive and recaptured.

They were wise in the ways of prison camp life. All were great scroungers, magnificent conversationalists, and adept in the techniques of German-baiting. Like all "old prisoners," their many months of confinement, along with their period of isolation in the mountains, had given them plenty of time to philosophize, daydream about the future and develop eccentricities. John Mayne, a Regular Army Commando and Veteran of the Dieppe and Tobruk raids, planned to emigrate to Australia. Peter Foulsham would return to London and study law. Howard Davies would come to the States, buy a Packard roadster, return with it to Rhodesia and write animal stories. Richard Edmonston-Low, the Canadian, would seek his future in New Mexico. Keith Esson longed to return to Christ Church in New Zealand and open a bookstore. Lock Creighton would go back to Edinburgh. Kalvan Singh planned to stay in the Army and become a general, as did Athon Naravane. Dudley Saker, whose father was Director of Education for

India's Central Provinces at Nagpur, would enter the Diplomatic Corps. They all had interesting stories to tell.

On leaving Siena, our visions of traveling through Northern Italy in troop-train fashion disappeared when a 14-car freight pulled into the siding. Lieutenant Colonel Trendel, the ranking officer in our group, insisted that as officers we be kept together. He demanded special accommodations from the German train commander. After much loud argument, the 30 of us were given a boxcar to ourselves, and, as concession to comfort, the bare flooring was covered with fresh straw. As all other cars were strawless and packed with 50 prisoners, we considered our lot fortunate.

Even with 30 men, there is not much room to spare in a small European boxcar. Each of us staked out a small bit of wall space as our own, but sleeping stretched out was an impossibility and had to be done in shifts. Our possessions, by now reduced to one knapsack or cloth bundle apiece, came in handy as backrests or pillows. (It was undeclared but understood that no one violated the territorial rights of his neighbors.)

We were locked in from the outside and the sliding door sealed shut. The only light within the car filtered in through slit-like vents near the roof at each end of the two sidewalls. With a boost, a tall man could get an eye up to one of these and report on the outside world. But the view was so limited that it was hardly worth the effort. Once a day, usually in mid-morning, the train stopped on some isolated stretch of track, the doors were opened, and two or three carloads at a time were allowed out to stretch their legs and perform necessary evacuations within a watchful ring of armed guards. At these stops we were issued a bread ration for the day and given a canteen cup full of hot ersatz coffee.

Our food ration, issued initially for the entire trip, was one can of compressed meat per man. It was euphemistically labeled beef, but was unmistakably horse. We were cautioned by our companions to ration it to ourselves carefully. Most had experienced boxcar travel before on their way from the toe of Italy to Chianti. They knew that prison trains had the lowest rail priority, and that what might be one day's travel in distance, could well be a five- or six-day trip in time. They had learned also that hunger is the most powerful of man's instincts. No matter how great one's altruism, trying to appease a chronically empty stomach brings out all of one's selfish cunning, and it is fair game to take any advantage available.

As a result, we evolved a unique way of dividing our daily ration of three loaves of bread. We split into three groups of ten, each with a chosen representative. The three agents then drew straws to determine first, second and third pick of loaves. After the first day, second would move to first, third to second, first to last and so on in daily rotation. Each group of ten divided itself into two groups of five, again each with a chosen leader. The two leaders then alternated days of cutting the group's loaf in half; on the day when one cut, the other had first choice of the halves. Each group of five drew straws to determine the order in the cutting rotation on their half-loaf; when number one cut, number two had first choice and number one automatically got the last segment. Even with our ingenious system, the cutting ritual was intently watched, each man calculating which piece seemed the biggest and his chances of getting it. It was amazing with what micrometer precision the last-choice man could divide a loaf.

We adjusted quickly to our cramped existence. No experience is entirely bad if it can be shared in common with others. We talked and dozed and slept without much regard to time of day. We discovered a few dried tobacco leaves mixed in with the straw; cut up and rolled in newspaper, they were enough to make five community cigarettes, which we shared ceremoniously. We learned to interpret the sounds of the wheels, and the creaks, groans and clanks of the ancient wooden car. We were stopped more often than we were moving. Occasionally we waited for hours on some siding for other trains to pass. Our route took us through Florence and Milan. One night we were halted in the rail yards beyond Bolzano long enough to be bombed by our own planes. (Jerry Perlman and Bob Schlisler, the two teenage American flyers, insisted indignantly that the raiders could only have been British.) On the morning of the fourth day we did get to see the Alps at a stretch-stop above the Brenner Pass. It was frustrating to know that neutral Switzerland was only a few miles away. But snow still covered the ground, and the wind and cold were so severe that we were happy to load back into our car where straw and body heat could warm us again.

Our journey ended undramatically at Stalag VII-A, a large, long-established camp filled with prisoners from all nations. There, a few miles north of Munich in the town of Moosburg, endless rows of bleak, wire-enclosed barracks awaited us. Yet to all of us, the prospect was appealing. The prisoner of war lives only from day to day to day. Food, a bath, warmth and a straw palette bunk of our own lay ahead. Tomorrow would take care of itself.

Singing Strings at Sagan
Originally published November 1964

TWENTY YEARS AGO this month we were walking along a cobblestone road toward the small rail station in Sagan, a village in Silesia. Accompanying us was a bored and silent German soldier who intermittently pulled a bit of cheese and some sour, black bread from his metal canister and munched away in dispirited fashion. We were headed back to the ground force officer's Prisoner of War camp, Oflag 64, in Poland, about a two-and-a-half day journey under the conditions of rail travel at the time.

Since being captured on the Anzio beachhead almost nine months earlier, our supervised travel had taken us by supply truck to Rome, by motor lorry to a camp near Siena, by rail to Bolzano and Northern Italy through the Brenner Pass into Munich and a larger POW camp in nearby Moosburg. After a few weeks there we had traveled by rail again to the camp at Sczubin, a small Polish town near Bromberg.

For the first few weeks in Poland our spirits had remained good, but gradually over the next months the bare subsistence diet and steady preoccupation with thoughts of food along with the monotony of prison camp routine had dulled our consciousness to a low level of gray uniformity. When a request came for a medical officer to be sent to the large Air Force camp, Stalag Luft III, in Silesia, we had volunteered willingly. The change of scenery had only a temporary effect on brightening our outlook, and within a short time an overpowering depression, aggravated by the inactivity of close confinement and the frustration of holding daily sick-call with nothing to offer the ailing (most of whom were malingerers fighting the same boredom as we) settled in for good. In November when the opportunity came to leave Luft III and return to the camp in Poland, we had seized it but with little hope other than that change of any kind would be welcome.

At Sagan we had lived in a low, one-story, wooden-frame barracks within the main barbed-wire enclosure, but separated by more barbed wire from the three main compounds of the camp. Our medical lazaretto housed a medical and a dental treatment room, living quarters for three medical officers, one dental officer, several enlisted medical orderlies and about a dozen two- and four-bed rooms for the hospitalization of nonsurgical patients. Any cases of serious illness or those requiring major surgical treatment that we picked up at our routine sick-calls had to be sent to a larger prison camp hospital about 30 kilometers away, which served several camps in the general area.

One of the factors contributing to our discomfort at Luft III was the other American medical officer there. (The senior medical man and the dentist were both British.) He was a young First Lieutenant, loud, brash and typical of a personality later to be described as "the Ugly American." Although he had been in the Army only two months and in combat for less than a week before being captured in the wadis of North Africa, he was an authority on military tactics and a severe critic of the way the Allies were conducting their campaign against the Germans. In kriegie terminology he was also an "operator" who utilized the meager added privileges of his position as a doctor (protected personnel along with dentists, chaplains and war correspondents under the Geneva Convention) to his best advantage.

Using a hoard of rations, clothing and medicines culled from the extras in the medical parcels supplied by the Red Cross for hospitalized patients, he lived in relative comfort through barter and bargaining with the Germans. He enjoyed such seldom-seen items as cigars, loaves of white bread, wine and special cheeses and had amassed a large souvenir collection of rings, watches, cameras, laces, linens, china and other odds and ends that turned up sporadically in black-market transactions. There was little compassion in his nature, and his dedication to medicine was predicated only on its usefulness as an occupation of status adaptable to personal advancement. He had welcomed us enthusiastically when we arrived at Sagan, but with a slight reservation since our rank as captain was a step higher than his own as lieutenant.

It was logical that the two Americans should room together, and for several weeks we shared quarters pleasantly in spite of our differences in outlook. The aggravation that finally broke up our close association as roommates arrived one day in the form of a violin. It had been bargained for through one of his several civilian contacts and represented an outlay of some long woolen underwear, a pair of GI shoes, two packs of American cigarettes and a can of powdered milk.

Before long we discovered that our roommate was a far better businessman than he was a musician. He could sing only in a monotone, had little conception of rhythm or harmonies and in fact was almost completely atonal. As a boy of 8, however, the violin had been inflicted on him unsuccessfully for six months, and in maturity he had often regretted "not keeping on with his music." He regarded the violin as a great prize and attacked it with a ruthless determination, picking up where he had left off in his practice some 20 years before. Apparently he had never gotten much beyond the finger exercises and a halting rendition of Humoresque, but he was methodical and persistent and devoted two hours each afternoon and one hour each night to the instrument. Being tone deaf must have helped, since the noises and scrapings he produced were indescribable; they were also intolerable to normal ears.

After a week of tortured listening and getting no reaction to our hints that perhaps the violin was a faulty one, the rest of us agreed that some action was imperative. At the insistence of the British dentist who lived in the adjacent room and who was an accomplished accordion player, we prevailed finally through persuasion and military rank and moved the offending instrumentalist into a small patient room at the far end of the barracks. There he continued to saw away daily. This turned out to be an effective means of shortening the hospital stays of patients, for only the hardiest of our malingerers were willing to remain on the sick list for more than a couple of days thereafter.

As we walked away from Stalag Luft III that day in November, the violin noises at the start of another afternoon practice session filled the air and followed us down the road. Our German guard stopped eating his bread and cheese momentarily, shook his head in helpless dejection and muttered to no one in particular, *"Ach, Goth! Krieg ist besser."*

OFLAG DIRECTORY

Continued from previous issues

ALABAMA
Carey Demott
2930 Dartmouth Ave., Bessemer

ARIZONA
James Carpenter
227 North Mount Vernon St., Prescott
Preston Hogue
2249 E. 2nd St., Tucson

CALIFORNIA
Peter Gaich
525 N. Kingsley Drive, Los Angeles
James Hannon
574 N. Sunnyslope, Pasadena
Paul Johnston
4760 Idaho St., San Diego
James MacIsaac
39 S. Kalorama St., Ventura
Donald Roberts
5043 Mount Royal Drive, Los Angeles
Patrick Teel
1837 N. Alexandria Ave., Hollywood
Osie Turner
Rt. 2, Box 113-B, Escalon
Herman Volheim
710 Superba Ave., Venice
Howard Wallis
Rt. 1, Box 648, Denair

COLORADO
Patrick Trainor
Ordway

CONNECTICUT
Rudolph Malchiodi
29 High St., Deep River
Nicholas Rahal
8 Chichester Place, Danbury

DISTRICT OF COLUMBIA
Harvey Ford
2511 Que St., N.W., Washington
James Godfrey, Jr.
2505 13th St., N.W., Washington

Max Gooler
The Adjutant General, Washington
Marcellus Hughes
3808 Alton Place, N.W., Washington
Donald May
2208 Wyoming Ave., N.W.,
Washington 8
Clarence Melteson
4211 River Road, N.W., Washington
Louis Morgenrath
1210 — 12th St., N.W., Washington
Alfred Moss
The Adjutant General, Washington
John Waters
3900 Tunlaw Road, N.W., Washington 7

GEORGIA
Collins Kendrick, Jr.
374 Orange St., Macon
Arthur Mallory
LaGrange
William Shuler, Jr.
1007 2nd Ave., Albany

IDAHO
Reid Ellsworth
166 Taft Ave., Pocatello
Kenneth Speas
Shelley

ILLINOIS
William Cool
343 West Censer St., Paxton
Thomas Johnson
502 Greenwood Av., Kenilworth
Tom MaGee
912 So. 3rd St., Springfield
Owen McGee
1405 S. Euclid, Chicago
James Schmitz
804 Illinois Ave., Ottawa

INDIANA
Francis Habig
1105 No. Main St., Jasper
Carl Kasper
1210 Condit St., Huntington
William Morris
4325 Winthrop Ave., Indianapolis

IOWA
Richard Davis
10 Achre Apts, Fort Dodge
Duane Smith
General Delivery, Colfax

KANSAS
Norman Alloway
Rt. 1, Edna
James Halstin
5639 West Maple, Wichita

KENTUCKY
James Dew
Calvert City
Robert Watt, Jr.
Tates Creek Pike, Lexington

LOUISIANA
Howard Charlton
1366 Scenic Highway, Baton Rouge
Peter Graffagnino
2814 S. Carrollton Ave., New Orleans
Harry Picou
Montegut Rte., Houma

MARYLAND
William Bond
406 American Bldg. Baltimore
Martin Upperco
706 Oldhome Rd., Raspeburg

MASSACHUSETTS
Edward Humphrey
Rochester

Camp directory (partial) appearing in the October 1944 issue of The Oflag Item, *newspaper published by prisoners of Oflag 64 (officer's camp), Sczubin, Poland*

Winter Scene, 1945
Originally published March 1965

OUR MILD PRESENT winter recalled the memory of a contrasting one 20 years ago. At that time our enforced domicile was Barracks 8A, Oflag 64, the German prisoner-of-war camp at Sczubin, in what used to be the old Polish Corridor. The winter months at a latitude of 54 degrees have some fairy-tale qualities, but most of them are better appreciated outside the confines of barbed-wire enclosures. When good weather prevailed, the days were crisp and clear but remarkably short. Darkness persisted until well past nine in the mornings and returned again by four in the afternoon. Snow was everywhere, and, in the rural village setting near which we were penned, there was a quiet beauty and hush that blanketed and obscured even the drab realities of a prison compound. The nights offered spectacular lightings of the dancing aurora borealis here at this proximity to arctic regions.

In late January of 1945 we were concerned less with the beauty of our surroundings than with the prospect of imminent liberation from our prolonged confinement. The German war effort was collapsing, and the eastern front had disintegrated before the Russian advance. The German garrison that was guarding the nearly 2,000 American officers in Oflag 64 was increasingly apprehensive about its own safety since the foremost salient of the Russian push was aimed almost directly at our camp. Worry was evident on the faces of our captors, and their preoccupation resulted in considerable relaxation of camp routine and discipline. We kept an operational map of the European fronts posted on the bulletin board in the main administration building, and whereas earlier we had always been careful never to alter it except in conformity with official German releases, then we were openly changing the battle lines once or twice daily in accordance with the BBC bulletins received over our clandestine radios. The German guards and officers were frequent visitors to the board, apparently trusting our information more than their own news reports, which inevitably proclaimed heroic battles and great German victories stemming the barbaric Russian advance.

As the Russians drew nearer and the sound of distant artillery could be heard for the first time, there was great rejoicing within the camp. Within a few days we confidently expected to see the Russian tanks and vehicles appear, the camp gates opened, and our careers as prisoners ended. But for most of us, it did not happen that way.

Twenty-four hours before the calculated arrival of our liberators, the German garrison, on orders from Wehrmacht headquarters, clamped down on discipline, assembled the prisoners and announced that for our protection they were evacuating us to a safer camp near Berlin. Only the sick and incapacitated were to be left in the camp. With two German doctors supervising, the American doctors (there were over two dozen of us by this time) were instructed to hold sick-calls and weed out all prisoners who were unfit to march.

In the hurried preparations for evacuation; there was great confusion and much indecision among the prisoners. Try to stay in the camp or march out? Since the Russians were our great buddies at the time, all of us would have preferred to stay. But there was also the uncertainty, not only of what might be in store, but of a possible desperate German reaction and reprisal (they still had all the guns) if confronted with a general revolt and uprising of the prisoners. After surviving one to three years of prison camp existence, there was a hesitation on the part of many of us to jeopardize our own personal survival by some heroic but premature resistance that could result in disaster. Especially with the end of the war in sight.

Many of the prisoners did choose to feign illness and turned up on the sick list. In the confusion, and in addition to the truly ill and bed-ridden (among whom was war correspondent Wright Bryan, managing editor of the Atlanta Journal), we were able to leave over one hundred "sick" officers in camp along with five or six doctors to care for them.

On the morning of January 21, the rest of us marched out. A holiday picnic atmosphere prevailed as we assembled in the bitter cold and gray light of morning and started through the opened barbed-wire gates. The temperature was 16 below zero, and we were bundled up in all of the clothing we owned, layer on layer and of countless variety, to the limit of what could possibly be worn and still permit motion. Most of us had knapsacks or lugged wooden suitcases, and, in addition, blanket rolls containing other possessions were slung over a neck or shoulder. Some had fashioned makeshift sleds of tin can strips and wooden bed slats, which they pulled behind them, piled high with canned food and odds and ends. POWs are like pack rats, and everything we had ever saved, accumulated, scrounged or made from scraps and empty food tins was draped on our coats or dangled from some pocket, belt or button.

We headed south initially, and the march (which for some of the group eventually covered 234 miles in 60 days) began briskly. Although we marched in platoon groups stretched out in long columns of two abreast, our appearance was anything but military and certainly not in keeping with our status as gentlemen and officers. We were a ragged, attenuated horde straggling and shuffling along like an endless procession of decrepit refugees. The more literary among us were reminded of Tolstoy's description in *War and Peace* of the Napoleonic army's retreat from Moscow, except that in place of dejection and despair, our mood was one of excitement and anticipation. The snow lay everywhere, three and four feet deep over the fields and valleys with drifts reaching as high as eight and nine feet. The heavy, blowing snowfall of the night before had ceased, and the daylight was bright and clear under the hazy sun. The packed, dry snow on the uncleared, rutted roads screeched audibly under the tread of hundreds of marching feet, and our disorderly, strung-out procession, contrasting darkly against the brilliant white, looked for all the world like an unending, disjointed serpent, emitting smoke from every pore, shrouded in the misty haze of the condensing vapors of our labored breathing.

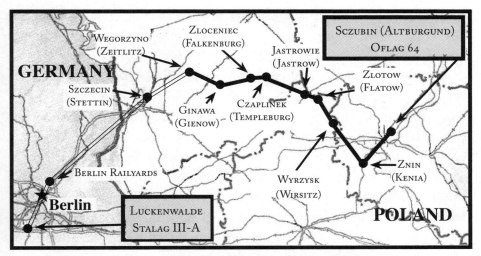

Oflag 64 to Berlin (Stalag III-A Luckenwalde)
Winter Scene March – January–February 1945

But as we said, there was no despair, only excitement. Our hopes and spirits were high, and no searing, penetrating cold that stabbed with every breath and numbed our hands and feet could change them. We were outside of our pen of barbed wire for the first time in months or years, on the open road, unconfined and unmolested by the dejected and miserable armed guards who marched beside us. The scenery was ever changing. We had no real idea about where our icy feet were taking us. But there was joy and jubilation. We were on the move and some-how, headed home.

Winter Scene (continued)
Originally published April 1965

As WE MARCHED out of the prisoner-of-war camp in Poland in the sub-zero cold of late January 1945, we knew little of our destination nor what the Germans planned for us. The march had been organized hurriedly by our German captors in an attempt to evacuate the camp before the rapidly advancing Russians could overrun it. Oberst Schneider, the portly, officious commandant of the German garrison and his executive officer, Hauptman Menner, a kindly and apologetic Viennese, bustled impatiently around the camp's barbed-wire gates until the last of the departing prisoners had cleared, and then sped off in their small battered car, scooting and skidding past the marchers to reach the head of the column. The only other transportation available, a decrepit wood-burning truck that followed the column, carried on its open-back platform, supplies and mess equipment, along with a dozen or so grumbling guards to serve as relief relays for those who marched beside us.

The countryside through which we moved was blanketed under deep snow, and, above a steely hoarfrost haze, the skies were bright and the air was quiet and still. We were bundled in clothing with our heads and faces swathed in makeshift hoods of blankets, scarves and sweaters, but the cold was still penetrating and bone-chilling. The condensing vapor of our breathing crusted in fine icy crystals on our lashes and eyebrows and along the edges of the woolen coverings over our mouths and noses. There was no way to crowd more than a few layers of socks into a pair of GI shoes and it was our feet that suffered most.

In contrast to the unhappy armed guards who slogged along beside us, we were in high spirits. Most of us were burdened under packs and blanket rolls loaded with an accumulated hoard of canned and packaged food that we had squirreled away over the months from Red Cross parcels for just such an emergency. On that first day of marching, however, the discomforts of our staggering loads and chilled bodies were counteracted by the excitement of being out from behind barbed wire and on the open road again. The terrain was new, and our interest in the changing scenery was keyed to a fever pitch of alertness by constant speculation about opportunities to take off on our own and escape.

We headed south initially in the general direction of Poznan, a rail-center about sixty-five miles away, but after covering about six miles, our direction was abruptly changed to west, and then again in a short time, to north. Oberst Schneider, scouting on ahead in his car, had learned that the Russians had cut across below us.

For the next seven days we marched, covering 10 to 18 miles a day. There was no let up in the cold, but the weather remained favorable with only an occasional light snowfall. We traveled mainly on the secondary rural roads, over a zigging and zagging route, northward and westerly, our direction changing from day to day according to the whim of Oberst Schneider and the reports he received on his scouting excursions ahead of the column. It was evident that the whole area was in a state of confusion. At times, and particularly on the larger highways, we encountered streams of civilian refugees moving in the same direction as we; at other times they passed us in the opposite direction.

Znin, Wyrzysk, Kenia, Szamocin, Schneidemühl, Krojanke and Zlotow—we moved through towns, villages, farm settlements, many of them almost deserted and nearly all of them with strange, tongue-twisting Polish names. We slept outdoors on straw piled on the snow, in barns, abandoned farm homes, warehouses, meeting halls, cattle pens, deserted barracks, whatever shelter was available in the vicinity when night came. We ate of our hoarded supplies of personal food, the daily ration of sour, black bread (Goon bread, to the POWs) and the occasional tinned beef issued to us by the Germans. At the end of a day's march there was sometimes a dipperful of watery stew, compounded from vegetables, barley and horsemeat, doled out by the Germans into whatever containers we had.

As the days passed we marched more grimly and determinedly. The enthusiasm and expectations of the first days on the road had dulled and disappeared in our fight against constant cold, fatigue and hunger. Each morning as we were reassembled and moved on, a group of fifty to one hundred prisoners were left behind. Old infirmities and war wounds, sickness and plain exhaustion took its toll on men already undernourished and unaccustomed to prolonged exertion after the months or years of prison inactivity. By far the greatest incapacitating ailment was the recurrence of old trench foot and frostbite. The Germans allowed one or two of the doctors to remain with the group left behind; more than two dozen of us had started with the column.

All during the march we walked with Arthur Mallory, our double-decker bunkmate for the past five months at Sczubin. Mallory, a Citadel graduate, had been a company commander in another regiment of our own 45th Division and had been captured in the same convulsive battle on the Anzio beachhead almost a year before. Every night, whether huddled together in the straw piles, burrowed into a haystack or sheltered in some barn, we argued the merits of leaving the column, joining a sick group or hiding out. But by day we were always marching again. There was safety in numbers. There was some compulsion too. Even though our hands were blue and numb, our feet frozen, our limbs exhausted, we were determined to walk as long as others were walking. There was also a medical conscience that would not let us abandon the men and the two or three remaining doctors who still marched with the column. Although there was nothing we could do medically for the sick ones, we were conscious that continued presence of even one sorry, unmilitary pill roller somehow boosted morale of the others.

Once at nightfall we were herded into the barns and outbuildings of a large estate at Charlottenburg. The manor house, a spired and turreted mansion with gingerbread gables and piazzas, set in an icy wonderland of snow and crystalled trees, shimmering in cold blue moonlight, looked like a fantasy from an Anderson fairy tale. With Mallory we lined up for chow, the inevitable thick barley soup that was being measured out from a makeshift kitchen under a porte cochere of the main house. Somehow the two of us slipped unnoticed into the house itself. We ate our porridge in an elegant music room, lavishly furnished in Victorian style, and after eating, set out to explore some of the ground floor rooms. In the library we came unexpectedly upon a group of unfamiliar German officers busy over maps. We identified ourselves and, on a pretext of some official nature, requested permission to look through the house for drugs and medicines. Whether it was our boldness or the Germans' preoccupation with their own worsening predicament, we were allowed to go on.

We slept that night on the thick rug of a drawing room floor, and no feather bed could have felt better. In our exploration, we had discovered three more levels above us with enough rooms, closets and passages to hide a hundred men. We debated long and hard that night whether to conceal ourselves and hide out, and in the end had fallen asleep, undecided. In the morning we rejoined the others and marched on.

By the ninth day we had covered over one hundred miles, and less than eight hundred of us were still marching. The skies were leaden, the winds biting, and as we marched the snow flurries increased. In mid-afternoon we were struggling forward against a howling blizzard, and the cold was almost paralyzing. The country was flat and open, and there was no protection from the blowing, driving snow.

For miles there was nothing behind to which we might return and, as far as we knew, no hope of shelter ahead. We kept moving slowly, and just as our endurance was at its end, we came upon an unnamed hamlet, a group of four or five deserted farm cottages lined along each side of the road. We stumbled into the unexpected haven, overcome with exhaustion and relief.

We were divided into groups and billeted in the houses. In a short time we had a fire going in the open hearth and had foraged and found enough stored vegetables and potatoes to concoct a hot mush. After eating we stretched out on the bare, earthen floor in front of the fire and slept. The blizzard raged on outside and finally subsided during the night, but none of us knew it. We slept a sleep of the dead. It was the most comfortable night we had passed since starting the march.

When we awakened in the morning, there was none of the usual noise and bustle of previous mornings; no clatter of hob-nailed boots, no prodding with gun-butts, no shouts of *"Raus!"* or *"Schnell!"* The new snow had stopped, and as we poked about, cautiously at first and then with more boldness, we discovered that our German guards were gone.

During the night, Oberst Schneider and his weary, dispirited men had pulled out and deserted us. We were free.

We spent the day organizing and planning. Food parties discovered and rounded up some pigs and chickens, and kitchen details went into action and prepared a feast. With a day of welcome rest, food and warmth, our fatigue disappeared and our enthusiasm returned. Unfortunately, there was no place to go. We were isolated in a vast expanse of winter wasteland in the middle of nowhere. The weather was colder than ever before with the temperature almost 30 below zero. We reasoned that, since the Germans had deserted us, the Russians must be close by, and therefore our best bet was to remain where we were and wait to be found. So we stayed.

With nighttime came the sound of motors, and we hurried out of the houses. Our Russian vocabulary was limited to two words, *Tovarich* and *Vodka*, and we were eager to use them. Our jubilation was short-lived, however; the Germans had come back. Oberst Schneider had run afoul of a motorized SS Latvian unit and had been made to return to take us back into custody. He was frightened and almost apologetic; with him this time were fresh troops and an SS Major who did not smile. We remained in the houses again that night, but once again as prisoners.

The brief taste of freedom, however, had stirred the prisoners. Some were rebellious and unruly, and a few skirmishes broke out between the men and guards. Although there were enough of us in each house to overpower the few armed troops who guarded us, again caution prevailed. The end seemed too near. We had come too far and had survived too long, to risk it. There were some impulsive ones, and there were some bitter ones, half-crazed with disappointment, who resisted. From this house or that one, an occasional pistol shot or the rattle of an automatic weapon kept us awake most of the night. We left a handful of wounded and three or four dead when we marched away in the morning.

When the marching group, with some aid from a shuttling truck, reached Stettin some days later, we were quartered in marine barracks on the shore of the Dammacher See. We were given a day or two of rest, but even so, when it was time to resume the march, there were almost 150 men who could not continue. Along with Lieutenant Colonel David Gold, we were the last two doctors with the group. He assigned us to remain with the 150 whom the Germans had agreed to move by rail. The rest marched on, and Colonel Gold marched with them.

The next day we were taken by truck to the rail yards and loaded into two cars, a slatted boxcar for cattle, and an open coal car for which a tarpaulin covering had been provided. The accommodations were crowded and not very luxurious, but it was better than walking. We were headed for Berlin, and although Stettin is less than one hundred miles north of the capital, we were four days reaching the rail yards there—the German rail system was having its problems at that time. We marveled then, and have since, at the obstinacy and unreasoning discipline of the German mentality that was concerning itself with moving two carloads of prisoners while its homeland was disintegrating around it.

In the Berlin rail yards, our two rail cars sat out three days and nights, back in the almost forgotten sounds of war. There were day bombings and night bombings, and some of the nighttime fireworks were spectacular displays. Miraculously there were no hits or near-misses in the vicinity of our sidetrack. And then one day we were moving again.

Our final destination was Stalag III-A, the large central collecting camp at Luckenwalde, about 40 miles southeast of Berlin. It was there that the Germans were funneling all of the prisoners evacuated from the many camps in East Germany. It was there, almost four weeks later, that Colonel Gold and the battered remnants of the original walking column arrived, still on foot. And it was there where we sat and waited for the war in Europe to end.

The Rail Yards of Berlin
Originally published February 1980

I N February 35 years ago we were walking, some one thousand American prisoners of war, across the frozen plains of Northern Poland. Our German hosts had evacuated Oflag 64, the American ground-force officers' camp near Bromberg, a scant 24 hours before the rapidly advancing Russians overran it. Presumably the idea was to "save" us from the barbaric Russian army, but probably there was also some imagined bargaining value in retaining us as prisoner-hostages under German control as the war's end approached. All of us would have preferred being left in the camp to await liberation by our then Russian allies, but the Germans had the guns and we were in no position to argue.

Actually, we did leave about a hundred or so prisoners in the camp—infirmary patients, some doctors, men who couldn't walk or who feigned illness and a group of others who hid out in the half-dug, escape-tunnel projects or somehow managed to get lost in the confusion of the hurried departure.

As we walked, day after day, the marching column grew smaller and smaller. We were not properly clad to withstand continuous daily exposure to such unremitting cold temperatures—that ranged from 40 below zero during two days of blizzard winds up to a warmer 10 below on milder days. We wore regular government-issue woolens and overcoats, supplemented by odds and ends of sweaters, combat zoot-suits, knitted caps and gloves, and makeshift head and face coverings of blankets and whatever else we could salvage from our meager prison possessions. Unfortunately, our feet gave the most trouble; there was no way to keep them warm in regular GI shoes, which could not accommodate more than one or two extra pairs of socks. Consequently, each morning as the march progressed, after sleeping out in ditches, haystacks, or in deserted, unheated barns and sheds, there were always 30 to 40 men with frozen feet who could walk no longer and who had to be left behind to whatever fate awaited them.

After 14 days of marching, about half the column made it to Stettin, some 160 miles away toward the west. We left the column there to look after another hundred men who had an accumulation of ailments and infirmities. Later we were moved with them in two small rail cars (one a slatted cattle car, the other an open coal car) to the Berlin rail yards, and, after a few stationary days there, we moved again to Stalag III-A, the large collecting camp at Luckenwalde some 30 miles south of the capital. What was left of the walking column, which continued on from Stettin, eventually turned up, still on foot, at Luckenwalde three weeks later.

There were about 50 of us packed into each of the rail cars, which sat for two or three days and nights on a siding in the Berlin rail yards. Routinely, every night, the Allied planes came over and plastered the rail yards with bombs. Most of us, confined in the cars except for two short relief-function periods morning and evening under the watchful eyes of armed guards, were resigned to the hopelessness of our predicament. It became a matter of enduring another terrifying night huddled together, hoping the bombs would miss our siding and praying that sometime soon the cars would get moving again toward a safer location. Immobilized by self-concern, we were too cold and numb and intimidated to do more than suffer silently and hope to stay alive.

It was an experience in cold and hunger and misery that few of us have forgotten. However, all of this rather long introductory description (most of which was recorded in a couple of *Bulletin* articles back in 1968) serves only as background for an amusing story to illustrate that one man's memory of and reaction to the same experience do not always coincide with those of another.

Last year, talking to and comparing notes with another former POW who marched in that same column out of Oflag 64, we were surprised to discover that he, too, remembered the two cars and the nights in the rail yards of Berlin. He wasn't in the coal car with us, but in the other open cattle car. Sure, he remembered being cold and miserable too, but wasn't it a wild and hilarious time?

Wild? Hilarious?

John, who might easily have stepped out of the television cast of Hogan's Heroes, was a happy, extrovertish first lieutenant then; a manic, wheeler-dealer type who had spent most of his time back in the prison camp horse-trading cigarettes for food and whatever else caught his fancy. He was one of the rare ones who stayed busy constantly during his year of captivity, never seeming to have a depressed moment. Before leaving the camp, and in preparation for the march, he traded everything he possessed back into tobacco, filling his backpack and pockets with cigarette packages and stuffing many more into the space between his combat coveralls and his woolens beneath to the point where he could barely waddle. He still had a good supply left by the time we reached Berlin.

When darkness came and while the rest of us were hunkering down in fear and wishing the night would end, John had bribed his guards with cigarettes and was on the loose wandering all over the rail yards. He looked for German troop trains and when he found one would boldly climb aboard and parade up and down the aisles, a vendor hawking his wares in atrocious German, trading cigarettes to the German GIs for bread and cheese and jam and schnapps. No one seemed to mind his audacity, not even the one indignant German officer he ran into who wanted to know what the hell was going on and booted him off his troop train. But not before an exchange of liverwurst for two packs of cigarettes.

So you see, even a bleak experience has its lighter moments. It may all go to prove that misery is what you make of it, and that it helps to be born with a little self-confidence and a sense of the ridiculous.

March 1945: Luckenwalde
Originally published March 1971

R EADING THE EXAGGERATED prose of militant minority spokesmen and their liberal sycophants, as they describe oppression, hunger and disgraceful living conditions throughout America, sometimes makes us wonder if they can really be serious. They seem unaware that freedom and comfort (health even) are relative commodities. Even after 25 years of indulgent living during a period of unprecedented affluence, it still isn't difficult to recall how it once felt to live an oppressed and regimented life under utterly miserable conditions in the prison camps of Germany as World War II neared its end.

By that time, most of us who had been prisoners for a year or more accepted crowding, primitive sanitation, constant cold and gnawing, chronic hunger as a regular part of existence. We knew—or at least we hoped—the war would end eventually and a better future lay ahead. But there was always a feeling of helplessness and an uncertainty of how it might end in particular for us individually. It didn't pay to plan beyond the next tomorrow.

For the 130 of us who arrived at Luckenwalde's Stalag III-A, 35 miles south of Berlin, early in March 1945, just the prospect of sleeping under a roof again seemed fortunate. We had survived a two-week march across northern Poland in howling blizzards and temperatures of 20 and 30 below zero. We had endured a long eight days of rail travel from Stettin (now Szczecin), half of us jammed into an open-slatted cattle car, half in a coal gondola covered by a torn tarpaulin. So, shelter—a straw pallet of our own to stretch out on and the comparative warmth of barracks life—was an unexpected windfall.

Viewed from more fortunate times, Luckenwalde was an incredible experience for thousands of Allied prisoners. As the Russians advanced, the string of prison camps in East Germany and Silesia was abandoned, and prisoners, on foot until they could march no longer, were funneled westward toward Stalag III-A. By March, with over 17,000 men of all nations there and more arriving daily, the already overtaxed camp organization was completely overwhelmed. More than 4,000 newly arrived American enlisted men were living on bare ground covered only by soggy straw under six, circus-type tents on a mud-and-snow-swept clearing. One large open-pit latrine and one water point served them all. By contrast, as officers, we lived in luxury, sleeping on bunks in barracks and with two aborts (latrine buildings) for our convenience.

The six barracks in our compound, occupied by Polish, French, American, British, Norwegian, Belgian and Serbian officers, were segregated by seven-foot, double barbed wire from the rest of the camp. About two hundred of us lived in the south end of Barracks XII, a long, one-storied, brick and wooden building, in a room one hundred by forty feet. There was a similar room at the north end and between the two was a washroom equipped with three stone troughs and two dozen iron spigots, which were eternally leaky, frozen or not working.

Three ceramic-tiled stoves about eight feet high were spaced down the long axis of our room. They were the heating system, but at this point there were no briquettes or coal to burn in them. Our bunks were heavy, three-tiered, wooden frameworks, built in sections of 12, each being two bunks long and two wide. The straw-filled mattresses of coarse fiber sacking, resting on four or five wooden bed slats, were odorous, dank and infested with lice, bed bugs and fleas contributed by countless occupants before us. (We added new crops of our own.)

We had rearranged the bunk sections into cubicles around a wooden table for 24 men, with a wooden stool for every two. Ratty lines of twine and string, stretched between bunks and rafters, were draped with washing and laundry that never dried. The dirt-and-soot-covered windows let in a minimum of light during the day, and, by night, the eight weak light bulbs dropped from the rafters (two or three were always burned out) glowed as dim blobs of orange in the smog-and-smoke-filled room.

Primarily, body heat kept us warm, but also our homemade tin can stoves (heatless smokers, we called them) in which we tried to burn scraps of cardboard, twigs and shavings from the bunks and bed boards, in an attempt to heat water or warm food undoubtedly helped. In addition, our fat lamps—tin cans filled with margarine, grease and a floating cloth wick, which we lit at night after the nine o'clock lights out—contributed something. The barracks atmosphere, at all times, day or night, was far thicker than any pea soup fog. To normal nostrils the odor must have been indescribable—a suffocating, miasmic blend of unwashed bodies, grease, sour food, dirt, smoke, filthy bedding and damp brick flooring. Periodic airings, even on windy, sunshiny days, had little or no effect on it.

Red Cross food parcels had ceased to exist, though most of us still had left, squirreled away, a few cigarettes, raisins and prunes, and some powdered coffee, tea and milk. Breakfast was at 7:30 a.m. when a tub of hot water arrived from the central kitchen. It consisted of ersatz coffee, a few soaked prunes or raisins and a slice of sour, black German bread pathetically "toasted" on a tin can stove. After roll call at 8:30, we policed the quarters, which meant straightening out the ragged, gray blanket on the straw pallet, sweeping the cubicle and airing the barracks as a gesture to health. The rest of the day was our own until the next roll call at 5:00 p.m. Lunch, the one German meal served each day, consisted of a dipperful of stew or soup made of cow bones; stringy horse meat; rotten cabbage; rutabagas and barley; six shriveled, boiled potatoes the size of walnuts, eaten through with black rot and worm tunneling; and another slice of bread with currant jam. For the evening meal, hot water, ersatz tea and bread again. At a generous estimate we managed about seven hundred calories a day.

Under such conditions there was not much we could do but exist. We accumulated sack time, we talked and swapped stories, argued and griped, played cribbage and cards, worked at tinsmithing. When the weather permitted, we walked outside within the limited confines of our barbed wire enclosure; sometimes we just stood on the rise next to one of the latrine buildings and watched in fascination the new,

German jet fighters, which occasionally whooshed by overhead. But mostly we planned menus; long, detailed 12-course meals that someday we hoped to eat again.

Sex was never a topic of conversation. We had discovered long before that it ranked far down the list of man's basic drives; we concluded that Freud had never been cold or really hungry. It was a depressing, monotonous, gray existence. Yet we were thankful to be there instead of still undergoing the hardships of the month before. In comparison to those in the other compounds of the camp, like our own enlisted men, the Italian forced-labor prisoners, and especially the Russians (in five years some 15,000 of them were said to have died at Luckenwalde in two typhus epidemics and from tuberculosis), we were a privileged minority. And, of course, all of us at Luckenwalde were infinitely better off than many displaced German civilians or the Jews, Poles and political prisoners in such camps as Buchenwald and Dachau.

Out of sheer perversity we wish, at times, that some of our loud, militant critics, the Huey Newtons, Cleavers, Seales, Hoffmans, Jane Fondas and Angela Davises, who find life in America so degrading and unbearably inhuman, could spend a year of living under ordinary prison camp conditions.

Part Four

POST-WAR RECOVERY

Introduction

The following chapter was discovered among the author's papers many years after his death. It is a remarkable description of his experiences and of his state of mind in the weeks following his arrival at Luckenwalde after being liberated from Oflag 64 in Poland.

Based on study of personal letters, it appears Dr. Graff put the handwritten document to paper within the first ten years after the end of the war. Composed several years before assuming his duties as Editor of *The Bulletin of the Muscogee County Medical Society*, Part Four represents his very first attempt to describe his wartime experiences.

He wrote in a stream-of-consciousness style, placing himself in the narrative as an observer and referring to himself only in the third person.

The episode takes us from a cold bare cell in a treatment facility somewhere in Germany or Belgium and dramatically documents the workings of a mind sinking in and out of sanity and consciousness. He describes a condition that would undoubtedly have been labeled "shell shock" in his day, or, in today's terminology, Post-Traumatic Stress Disorder.

The rather lengthy account wanders through details and lucid memories of his early life and ends abruptly with his transfer to a mental hospital in Texas during the summer of 1945. His return to the U.S. followed frantic and concerted efforts by family members to locate him after having been listed as "Missing In Action" for a period spanning several months.

His symptoms and condition were so severe he would subsequently undergo shock treatments to return him to a "normal" and productive life. Those who knew him during his nearly four decades of life after the war will be profoundly amazed to learn of the depth of his mental deterioration during this brief post-war interlude. Both the speed of his recovery and his ability to recall and later to describe the experience itself are truly remarkable. – R.D.G.

JAMES H. MORRISON
6TH DISTRICT OF LOUISIANA

HOME ADDRESS:
HAMMOND, LOUISIANA
WASHINGTON ADDRESS:
202 HOUSE OFFICE BUILDING
FLORENCE H. COOLEY
SECRETARY
PEGGY BURCAW
ASSISTANT SECRETARY

COMMITTEES
ROADS
LABOR
CLAIMS
CIVIL SERVICE
INVALID PENSIONS
PUBLIC BUILDINGS
AND GROUNDS

Congress of the United States
House of Representatives
Washington, D. C.

June 20, 1945

Honorable. Henry L. Stimson
Secretary of War
Washington, D. C.

Dear Mr. Stimson:

I have been advised by Dr. Peter Graffagnino of New Orleans Louisiana, that he has received no word from his son, Captain Peter Carl Graffagnino, O-425300, who was prisoner of war No. 3149 at Oflag 3-A, since February 1945.

Dr. Graffagnino has come to Washington for the purpose of endeavoring to obtain some information concerning his son and was successful in contacting several officers who were in the prison camp with his son and who have recently been liberated.

The circumstances surrounding Captain Graffagnino's case are most unusual and the information he received came from Lt. Colonel David Gold, 2014 Eastern Parkway, Schenectady, N.Y., who is now home on furlough since his recent liberation. Col. Gold and Captain Graffagnino were the only two American physicians in the above named prison camp until Captain Graffagnino became seriously ill with an extreme case of psychosis to such an extent that it was necessary for Col. Gold to request the German government to commit Captain Graffagnino to an institution. This incident occurred in March, 1945. Col. Gold states that the institution was located at Brandenburg, Germany which is about 40 miles south of Berlin. Colonel Gold immediately wrote the International Red Cross and the Swiss Legation requesting that they transfer Captain Graffagnino to an American hospital, but never received a reply. Captain Graffagnino has never been heard from since and all the internees have been liberated and returned to the United States.

Dr. Graffagnino and his family are frantic with worry over their son, not knowing whether he is alive or not, and it is my urgent request that the normal chain of the evacuation of the sick and wounded be set aside in the movement of this individual to the United States and that permission be granted for a medical aide to bring Captain Graffagnino to the States or for a relative to go overseas to accompany the officer. The father of Captain Graffagnino, who is a prominent surgeon in Louisiana, is very anxious and willing to go overseas and bring his son home. For your information I have been advised the following officers, who have been liberated and returned to the United States, were interned with Captain Graffagnino and can substantiate the information in this letter:

Col. Thomas D. Drake – Chief of Staff
Captain Kleystuber – (home) Glebe 4400, Ext 82
1st Lt. Alfred Mose – (home) Chestnut 4214
Lt. Col. David Gold – (home) 2014 Eastern Pkwy.,
Schenectady, N.Y.

I am sure you understand the urgency insofar as the time element is concerned in having this officer located and returned to the United States for immediate medical attention.

Your attention in this matter will be greatly appreciated by the family of Captain Graffagnino and the citizens of Louisiana as well as myself.

Sincerely yours,

James H. Morrison, M.C.

Reproduced to simulate original letter.

The Post-War Break With Reality
Previously unpublished

HE WAS HAVING a terrible time marshalling his ideas. Marshalling—good word, marshalling. Marshall Foch. Marshall Timoshenko. Martial music. Chump. Chump, chump the boys are marsh, marsh, marching. He beat the time with a closed fist against the marble floor.

He sighed and curled up in a tight little knot, hugging his knees to his chest and chin, making himself as small as possible, wedging into the corner of the cold empty room.

He tried to rest because somehow he knew he must, but he was distracted by the rhythmic beat of his own pulse. He relaxed his respiration and concentrated on slowing his heart rate and was pleased with the result. He had no watch, but he imagined he had gotten it down to around 50 beats a minute. He had practiced this many times before. Conscious control of the metabolic processes. Reduce oxygen consumption to a basic minimum; expend no energy. The secret of hibernation. He was in a state of complete suspension of animation. All except his mind, that unruly mind. It was racing and there was no stopping it. It had been racing for weeks now—or was it months? No matter. There were still problems to solve, truths to ferret out, myths to explode. Every thing was simple, every thing had an answer. Every single, conceivable thing that had happened in the world from the time of recorded history was explainable if you started with facts and applied pure, simple logic; pure cold reason. A equals B; B equals C; therefore, A equals C. Blip-blip-blip. He felt a kinship with those great minds of the past—Aristotle, Descartes, da Vinci. What a wonderful and awesome thing was the human brain!

With almost no effort he could recall any event that had ever happened to him, any incident that had ever impinged on his consciousness from the time of his first awareness. He could repeat long forgotten childhood conversations word for word. He could mimic his own childhood voice and give the replies of his playmates in their own voices with their own inflections, their own intonations.

He couldn't go back much beyond the age of 2, at least he hadn't been able to so far, although at times it seemed he could almost capture some vague impression of infancy—a smell perhaps, or the stiffened feel of cotton clothing with its dried crusting of soured milk.

They had moved from the house on DeSoto Street in the spring of 1918 when he was just 2 years old. He had seen it many times in his later life, but had never once been back inside. And yet he could remember the kitchen with its clean, scrubbed wooden flooring, the door on the right to the backyard steps, the wooden, white-enameled table and its heavy, white marble top with the fluted, scalloped edges.

"Get up. Get up. Why you don't get pneumonia is beyond me!" The voice of his angry, provoked mother came back to him. He used to like to lie prone on the floor, his head turned to the left, his eyes almost squinted shut, peering at the wood pattern of the door sill. There was always a twisted, grayish strand of mop string caught under a sliver of wood grain. He had liked the feel of the cool rush of air that blew in through the space between the door and the sill; he liked the musty wet wood and mop smell that was always there.

He remembered other things too from the early time. His father, gaunt, unshaven, still recovering from the almost fatal case of influenza; the steps down to the earthen-floored basement and the pattern of the floor joists beneath the house; the clawed, walnut feet on small brass wheels of the dining room table. All of this before they had moved to the new raised bungalow on Carrollton Avenue just before his second birthday. He had never had time to think about these things before. But they were all there, and more. And now he had time, and he had been busy, busy, busy, sorting out his life in detail, in painstaking, chronological order.

The power of total recall. There had been one or two of his professors who were supposed to have had it, but he wondered if they really did, at least to this extent. He himself had never had it before. Not until recently. He speculated perhaps that it was a capability of every human brain. He reasoned that every sensory impulse from whatever source, through whatever portal, for every fraction of a moment of man's lifetime, was recorded indelibly, biochemically, permanently. It took only a combination of the proper conditions to unlock the doors and release the flood.

He was struggling now to contain that flood. His thinking was clear, crisp, concise, logical, but my God, it was rapid. The rush of ideas, thoughts, came so fast—each suggesting four, five or six more— that it was difficult to sort them. Distractibility. Flight of ideas?

"True mania is characterized by a general sense of well-being, euphoria, elation, hyperactivity of the mind, distractibility and a flight of ideas." He could see the page and the print in the red copy of Strecher and Ebaugh as if it were lying here open before him. He could see old Watrous, disciple of Adolph Meyer, his old professor of psychiatry (who preferred the terms "psychobiology" and "psychopathology") standing there in front of the class, lecturing on tics and habit spasms, grimacing and tugging at his collar at rhythmic intervals.

"Watch out for those daydreams, Number 32; careful with those suspicions, Number 86; watch those temper outbursts, Number 41; don't let them throw you." Old Watrous would hold a conference with the class once a month in which he would hand out condensed nuggets of advice, gleaned from his reading of the interminable papers on self-analysis that they handed in by number instead of name. He had told them once that they were the damnedest bunch of introverts with the least self-confidence of any class he had ever taught. He smiled grimly, cynically to himself. *If old Watrous could see me now,* he thought. *Jesus!*

He was aware occasionally, when he took the time to look at himself, that his appearance must be unkempt, that he must be dirty. Even wild looking. How in hell could he be otherwise? His only clothing was a pair of tattered, rough cloth pajama pants. He was alone in a room that measured nine by twelve feet roughly—he had paced it off. It had four gray plaster walls, a ceiling with a single light bulb, a marble floor, a small window nine feet up on the wall and a heavy wooden door with a small aperture on the opposite wall. That was all. No stool, no bed, no straw—nothing. He must have eaten, he must have performed the usual excretory bodily functions, but for the life of him he couldn't remember where or when. It really wasn't that he couldn't remember, it was just that those things right now were unimportant. Too trivial to bother with. He was aware that he had been ill. He remembered open infected sores on his arms, legs. Not while he had been in this room, but in the first building in one of the other places. The German institution. He had licked them with his tongue, like an animal. Why not? It was the same principle as the autogenous vaccine, wasn't it? He knew that the staph or strept or whatever the organisms were might be inactivated by the gastric juice, but what else could he do? Something had worked. He was still alive, wasn't he?

He was aware too that there had been periods of delirium. Wild, raging, destructive episodes. He still retained a blurred mental picture of that first dark room he had been left in at the prison-camp hospital near Luckenwalde. Broken chairs, splintered bed, shattered glass, a goddamn shambles. His hands and wrists were covered with scars, some old, some new. Compulsion? Not really. He had just wanted to prove to himself that he could punch a fist through a pane of glass without hurting his hand. Velocity at impact was the secret.

He was even aware that he was insane. Not just plain nuts, but really insane. A full-blown humdinger of a case. He hadn't been able to classify the type completely. Manic? Manic-depressive? Paranoid?

Schizophrenic? It had to be one of them. Hallucinations? Delusions? Persecution complexes? He had had all of them.

And then there were periods like this one, when his mind was clear and sharp. Where every one of his senses—smell, sight, touch, taste, hearing—was so damned acute that it was unbelievable.

He derived a certain amount of strange satisfaction in the knowledge that this was happening to him, a person with a medical education and training. The overall awareness, the acuteness of perception the super-alertness—not only to external stimuli, but to his own bodily physiology—were fascinating to him. The knowledge that he could interpret these things scientifically kept him feverishly probing, searching, experimenting. He felt he had solved many problems, that he was close to great truths that would explain some of those mystical experiences in human history, explain the unexplainable, fathom the unfathomable.

He had reviewed his whole life over and over, in detail, from infancy to adolescence, through college, through medical school, through internship and residency. The Army, his experiences in combat, his capture, the prison camps in Italy, Austria, Silesia, Poland and Germany. Right up to the moment that it had happened—the break with reality. It had been sudden.

He laughed, remembering May, one of the first girls he had been "in love" with. Typical, voluble May, representative of her class—different, impulsive, moody, outspoken, debutantish—who spoke in exaggerations. "Don't you ever feel unbearably queer? Like you were going crazy? Like there was a fine, thin string that might suddenly snap?" He couldn't remember any audible snap, but the break had been abrupt. Yet from his medical knowledge he knew that there had been a forewarning. It could be charted distinctly, chronologically.

But the timing worried him. *Why had it happened when it did?* He could think of many moments along the way, moments of stress, where it could have occurred more logically.

Although he knew that a psychiatrist might nitpick through his early years and come up with something, there were none of the classical findings there. There had always been security, no broken unhappy home, no major catastrophes. He had always been a little shy; quiet and introspective yes—but he made friends easily; he liked people; people liked him. He had been smart, a good student always. Never a leading bookish brain, but always close to the top of his classes. Honors had come to him, and always with a measure of genuine surprise on his part. Not that he hadn't hoped for them, but he had usually felt that they were not quite deserved. In high school, as a senior, he had been named the best all around cadet, just for being better than average in many things, but excelling in none. Really. It was a year when the top athletes were unusually poor scholars, and the top scholars were dreadful athletes. A Phi Beta Kappa in college, even though he had gotten lost in physics and math. An AOA in medical school, even though he had stumbled through his senior year in a fog. Leadership fraternities. Interesting man on the campus. Long in conscience, short in confidence.

Had the seeds been present then? Had it begun in medical school?

He had known then for the first time that his mother was a classic case of cyclic mania and depression. Never severe enough for an institution, but typical nevertheless; never a break with reality like his own. But it had never caused him to worry about his own heredity, not then. The prolonged, tantalizing frustration of his almost one-sided love affair that carried on through medical school, hospital training and his first year in the Army had given him despairing moments, but he had survived them. In fact he remembered the surging feeling of relief when she had solved the problem for him by abruptly marrying someone else.

Had that been the start?

He remembered the phase, immediately afterward, when everything became enjoyable again, his outlook freshened. He remembered his own marriage some six months later to Jane. The courtship had been brief, impulsive with the typical urgency of the war, but there had never been doubt in his mind.

It had seemed to him that he had been abnormally calm during the wedding ceremony. Almost a detached observer, he had watched his best man fumble nervously to produce the ring. The minister, intoning what must have been hackneyed and commonplace phrases, had looked up to find him staring penetratingly, amusedly, and had muffed his lines in confusion. It had been a brief, strange interlude of alarming clarity that had left him wondering about thought transference.

Had that been the beginning?

Jane Drury and First Lieutenant Peter C. Graffagnino

Some months later, after a bout of influenza, the enthusiasm and interest that had swept him through a year and a half of army life, and five months of pleasant marriage, had suddenly waned. He had become silent, morose, dissatisfied. He had been able to carry out his required medical duties only by tremendous effort. It was an overpowering depression that he could not explain to himself or to his lovely, devoted new wife. Her own quiet unhappiness and puzzlement only served to deepen his concern. He had wondered then for the first time whether his mother's manic-depressive trait was part of his own inheritance.

Then, like magic, when the Division had sailed for overseas combat, the weight, the oppression had vanished. Interest, awareness, enjoyment returned. Almost exhilaration. There was a feeling that the slate had been wiped clean. What lay ahead was adventure, new lands, new experiences, danger perhaps. The uncertainty of the future was a challenge. He would enjoy it, make the most of it. He might never return. Never before had he felt so alive, so competent, so confident as he did during the months of combat. The Algerian coast, the invasion of Sicily, Salerno, Cassino, Anzio. He could recall in detail every day, every hour, every moment from the time the invasion craft had grated its keel in the shallow surf off the Sicilian beach. His sensibilities sharpened, his mind alert, like a fresh, bright fine sponge of infinite capacities, soaking up every experience, savoring every nuance. His drive, his cheerfulness and his enthusiasm were contagious, and the men of his own small battalion medical section had been devoted to him. For eight months— through heat and dust, rain, cold, mud, ice, snow, mountains, plains, sickness, destruction, devastation and death—he had moved onward and the men with him. A small unit on the fighting perimeter of a combat division, dealing out compassion and empathy, balm for the ailing, forgetfulness for the agonized wounded instead of bullets and mortar shells. And all of the time the eagerness and exhilaration had persisted—even heightened. It had been a wonderful experience.

His capture by the Germans had not dimmed his drive. Choosing to stay on to care for a group of wounded who could not be moved, he had had to order some of his section to leave him. He had felt almost like a little god picking the ones who were needed to stay and help—knowing that they would be captured with him. Even afterward, in the weeks on the German front lines, in the months of travel as a prisoner up through Italy, Austria, Silesia and finally into

Poland, there had been no despair, only continued interest, insatiable curiosity and enthusiasm.

And yet there had been intervals, even during those months—actually over a year from the time the Division had sailed—when he had been aware of an occasional personal disquiet. A consciousness that his verve and well-being were a little out of keeping, in conflict with the harsh reality of his surroundings. He remembered the sobering effect of an impromptu leave urged on him by the Battalion Commander. He and Buck, his driver, had taken a Jeep and driven back to Naples. It had been the first time he had been away from the front line, the troops, his own little world, in over five months. Sitting warmly and comfortably in the plush red velvet chairs of the opera house, fatigue had almost overcome him; emotion welled and he had found himself crying. Less than three hours before, they had left the mountainside above Venafro, soaked and cold, ankle deep in mud, a vista of shattered trees, crumpled stone huts, shell holes, mortar bursts, machine gun rattlings, artillery screams. The contrast had been too much, the change too rapid. He had looked around him over the packed, predominantly military audience. Who were all these people? How could they sit here in comfort only a few miles away from destruction? Buck had felt it too. With no words they had left before half of the performance was over. But once outside, the feeling had passed. They had enjoyed their three days in Naples. And they had gone back loaded with things—food, clothing, equipment—mostly stolen or requisitioned for their companions at the front.

Another time, during the many lulls of combat, he had been alone in one of the aid stations, a cleaned out rock and thatched animal pen high on the mountainside, and by the light of a flickering candle he had written a long and introspective letter to his father. Like many fathers and sons, there was deep affection between them, but there had always been difficulty in communicating. Neither had ever been a conversationalist. He had unburdened his soul; all of the unspoken things of a lifetime were poured onto the paper. In it he had wondered then about his recent cyclic phases in mood. But there had been no pattern, and he had concluded then that situational pressures and changes were responsible. Still he had not been sure.

Did it start then?

He was ignorant of religion. His father, embittered from a youthful humiliation with religion, of candle carrying on the event of his first communion, a gift-collecting round of the countless relatives, had never forgiven his devout, old-world mother and was violently anti-Catholic. A dislike that encompassed all religions as sham, hypocrisy. His mother's father, dignified, proud, retired sea captain, had lived with them and he had watched him die, adamant to the end that no priest should be called; his mother, caught in between, needed the crutch of religion.

Even so, he himself had been exposed. A year in Catholic school in first grade. (He still remembered an ogress of a nun to whom discipline was a cat and nine tails.) Several years of Sunday school in a Church of Christ. (He had gone with his bosom buddy and next door neighbor.) Episcopal Sunday services for many summers on vacations with a family he had been devoted to. Occasional forays into the Presbyterian and Catholic churches on Sunday dates. He had married in a Unitarian church. But he had had no background for religion; none of it had struck a responsive chord. He would not have called himself an atheist, agnostic perhaps. He didn't know. At times he envied some of his friends, some much more intelligent than he, their knowledge of religion and their faith. But he could not make himself believe, he could not make himself feel a need that wasn't there.

"There are no atheists in foxholes." In combat he had heard that old saw repeated many times, often by his own 2nd Battalion chaplain for whom he had had no respect—a hypocritical Holy Roller if he ever saw one; a Sunday chaplain; a righteous, God-fearing, cliché-spouting, psalm-singing misfit. He had tried to despise him, but he couldn't. Not even when the bastard had stayed away from the aid station for almost two months because they had had it set up in a pitiful mountainside chapel, obviously Catholic and under Papal jurisdiction. All he could feel for him had been pity. Poor ineffectual Raley; who could not communicate with the men; who tried with all his might to fit in, to be one of the boys; who had nothing to offer except his own weakness, his own fear of death and the Almighty. Poor Raley, who watched helplessly as his own flock, good, hard, rawboned Protestant Americans to the core, drifted away little by little, month after month to fall under the sway of genial, whiskey-drinking, card playing Father Barry, the 1st Battalion chaplain. How could he despise Raley? In his own compassion he had found himself drawing closer to him, bolstering his courage, shielding him from hurt, intervening, defending. Finally, just before they had come down from the miserable mountains in mid-winter, when he could see the last fibers of poor Raley's self-respect going slowly, when he himself could not stand the thought of being witness to the disintegration of faith in a man of God, he had evacuated him through medical channels. It had not been difficult. Everyone had trench foot.

Chaplain Father Barry leads prayer on Anzio

But he had no faith, no religion himself. And yet once on the Anzio beachhead, just before they had gone back in the line for their final fateful battle, he found himself standing in a grove of trees on a Sunday, apart, but edging closer, trying to be inconspicuous, as he watched Father Barry conduct Mass. The solemn mumbo-jumbo, over the cloth and paraphernalia spread on a Jeep hood, the personality of the man, the hush and wrapt attention of those cynical, weary, combat-coarsened men stirred something within him. Many were like himself, hesitant and on the fringes. He had knelt self-consciously, and wondered whether he was out of reach.

Could that have begun it all?

Or had it started earlier, after Salerno, when they had brought Blumberg back to the aid station? Happy Jock, lover of life, lover of women, the light of the army. Permanent second lieutenant, defier of convention, non-comformist, antagonist to authority, chronic goof-off. His goofy smile was still set on his lips, and the sniper's bullet hole neatly centered on his forehead. Permanent, final, second lieutenant Blumberg.

Or later in the caves at Anzio, with Viereck? How could one find the answer to something like Viereck? Always unshaven, always sloppy. Harvard graduate, classical scholar, hard-working, quiet, unassuming Viereck. Four-eyed, owlish Viereck. Battalion Intelligence Corporal since they had left the states. He had worked under Weiner until Weiner had collapsed with hepatitis; then under Unterberger.

Always pleasant, always distant. A brain in chains. If he was resentful, it was never apparent. If he had feelings, you never knew it. He did his work efficiently, thoroughly, competently. He accepted danger, night missions, sentry work without emotion. Invaluable Viereck. He spoke German fluently, interrogated all the prisoners.

He had tried to befriend Viereck, so had the others. And they were all friends, good devoted friends, even Viereck. But no one was close to him. No one maybe but Weiner, the loud, handsome Jew with the soul of Moses. What was it with Viereck? Shyness? A classicist's disdain for the rest of them? Reserve? Resentment? Torment? Whatever it was, it had ended there at Anzio in an artillery burst. Corporal George Sylvester Viereck, Jr., GI. No one had ever asked him about his father.

But he was off the track again. That's what happened to him in times like this when his mind was running off at a mile a minute. He held to his spot in the corner. Still immobile.

***

It had been well into summer there in the prison camp in Poland before the enthusiasm had disappeared. And depression returned.

He had reviewed a whole lifetime now. Childhood, high school, college, medical school, internship, residency, the army, the war—Sicily, Salerno, Cassino, Nettuno. He recalled that the new POWs from the western front spoke of it as the Anzio beachhead.

The Nettuno Debacle. The Battalion had gone up in the line on the night of his birthday [February 14]. It had taken positions astride the Albano road about two or three miles north of the overpass. Two days later the whole German Army massed for their all-out push to wipe out the beachhead with a drive down the axis of the Albano road. Eight days later what was left of the battalion was still there, two miles inside the German lines. Eight hundred men killed, lost, captured or wounded in action, all because of a new battalion CO, in combat for the first time, who didn't know when in the hell to pull out. When the handful of remnants had tried to fight their way back, he and some of his aid men had stayed on with the wounded.

Overpass at Aprilia – "The Flyover"

In his recollecting, it always took him awhile to get past Nettuno and the beachhead. It was the only thing in his combat experience that even resembled those stark, shell-pocked battlefields littered with dead, wrecked vehicles and crazy barbed wire entanglements that he remembered in the World War I movies of his childhood. He couldn't forget the wounded; he couldn't forget the hand-to-hand clubbing and bayoneting; he couldn't forget the pitiful peasants—old men, women, children—who huddled along with them in the caves as the artillery pounded night after night on the cave openings.

Pozzolana caves, scene of Battle of the Caves, February 1944

Every time the Germans stormed the cave openings, they all quaked together, waiting for the flame-throwers. Nothing could throw you into a panic like even a rumor of a flame-thrower. He couldn't forget the nobility and unselfishness that came out, even in some of the worst, sorriest soldiers. He wouldn't have spit on some of those battalion GIs in civilian life, but when the chips were down they were capable of greatness. It was as if all of the nonessentials had been stripped away, exposing the man and his naked soul. A few folded, of course, but the majority were magnificent. He couldn't forget old Eide, one of his corporals who crawled for a half hour from F Company's position through a steady artillery barrage and across fields of machine gun fire to get to the aid station in the caves. He came for more plasma and morphine. Three of them tried to hold him there in comparative safety until the firing would slacken, but they couldn't. He crawled out into the same hell with the supplies to get back to his own wounded. Within five minutes he had crawled back into the cave, a leg shattered, half of his face gone, crying because he hadn't made it back to his wounded who needed him.

Nettuno made him weep openly whenever he thought about it. At least the cave experience did. The rest was funny. His capture had been an anticlimax with comic-opera overtones.

He and Erich, the German aid man they had captured six days before, led a procession of litter cases out of one of the cave openings into the blinding, late-afternoon daylight, waving a Red Cross flag. It had almost worked, too. The procession had gotten about halfway to the Allied lines, passing busy German soldiers who were digging in, looking up only in curiosity, before they were stopped by a German major. His tank was in a shell of a ruined farmhouse. There followed a terrific argument through interpreters. Fielschmidt, the crazy Regimental Dentist who had led a rescue party on foot through the German lines with the Red Cross flag to reach them, was especially incensed. Red in the face and with his arms flailing wildly, he maintained this was a hell of a way to honor a truce. They were all noncombatants, they couldn't be captured. The argument seemed to last forever. The German major was impassive and adamant.

He had finally gotten Fielschmidt quieted down. The time was growing short because he knew, by way of the radio that had been left in the cave, that at dusk the Allied artillery was due to rake the whole area of the debate. The ridiculousness of the whole tableau hit him and the German major simultaneously—a forum on the ethics of warfare, on a stage set of carnage and destruction. They had both laughed and bowed. The column was turned to the left toward the road, accompanied now by some recruited German soldiers as guards. As they headed away, from the next rise, he had looked back. The major was still visibly shaking with laughter. Erich, the kindly German aid man (he had been an illustrator of children's books in civilian life), an ex-prisoner now, was back in the fold. He was standing stiffly at attention, as befit his corporal rank, next to the mirthful major. He waved goodbye to Erich.

Oflag 64, Sczubin (Altburgund), Poland,
drawing by POW Jim Bickers

"Alles ist besser in Deutschland" had been the refrain of the usually sympathetic captors all along the line of temporary camps since his travels as a prisoner had begun south of Rome. The compound at Sczubin (Altburgund to the Germans) had been a little better. It occupied the site—and some of the old buildings—of a boys' school, which had been converted by barbed wire enclosures, additional barracks, sentry towers into the main camp for captured, American, ground-force officers. He had lived in the old hospital building along with five other doctors, a dentist, the chaplain and Allen, the cynical war correspondent—protected personnel under the Geneva Convention, with the special privilege of an extra letter and postcard each week, and the theoretical possibility of repatriation. His enthusiasm had not dimmed during the

first months there, and he had busied himself with the minor medical duties assigned to him.

He had read incessantly. The hodgepodge of the camp library had yielded nearly all of Shaw and Ibsen, and some of Tolstoy, Dostoevsky, Schopenhauer, Goethe, Chesterton, Belloc, Wilde. He had had no stomach for the trivial. He had even tried the Bible, but had never gotten far. He found it unreadable.

But gradually, as he had seen it happen to many of the others there, the gray monotony of the endless days of prison-camp life, with the constant, incessant nagging of an empty stomach, had gotten to him. He had wondered then, cognizant of the intense preoccupation with food that colored the thoughts, dreams, plans of all of them, whether Freud had ever gone hungry. He could not ever remember any of them talking about sex. Hundreds and hundreds of men, hundreds and hundreds of bull sessions, and always food, food, food. When you stripped away the frills, it was survival, protection from the elements and food that counted. The stomach ruled the pelvis.

Increasingly he had found it more and more difficult to maintain a sustained interest in any activity. He had become morose, lethargic, uncommunicative, irritable. But it had not seemed too unusual at the time since he was one of many.

When the Germans had requested an American doctor to be sent to work at another camp, he had seized the opportunity and volunteered. Anything for a change. Anything to break the monotony. With a guard he had gone by train, but the eagerness and curiosity that had been part of him on the long travels up from Italy were gone. Nothing had stirred him. Even the carloads of starved human cattle, that had stood next to them on the sidings at Breslau for hours, had not penetrated his apathy. And it had become worse at Sagan.

He had lived in the revier, a bleak, one-story, wooden building in the medical compound that served as the infirmary for three of the vast air force prisoner compounds. He had joined another American doctor, a South African doctor and a British dentist. At first he had roomed with Barks, the American. Cocky, callous, unfeeling Barks, the personification of the great American tourist. Loud, insecure, self-centered, the product of mass education, dignified by a bar on his shoulder and an M.D. degree. One year out of medical school, one year in the army, three weeks after leaving the States, captured in Tunisia after his first four days of combat, Barks was an authority on military medicine, tactics and strategy. Barks had a full stomach, extra hospital rations, black-market deals on the side, cigarettes for bread, clothes for schnapps, integrity for cigars.

He had roomed with Barks, the violinist. Not since childhood had Barks had a violin, but now somehow he had had one again. Barks had no ear for music; he could not carry a tune, but he practiced methodically, daily, picking up where he had left off as a child. He had not improved. The grating, screeching sounds had been maddening.

The thing that had brought him to a breaking point, however, was not Barks so much as it was young Allen, a young bombardier, who had lain in the infirmary for months before he had arrived. Cheerful, uncomplaining. All under a cradled sheet, naked, the skin of his entire body desquamating, raw, weeping, with a chronic, exfoliative dermatitis. It never got better; day after day one area might heal, another would appear. Barks had lost interest, so he had taken over. There was nothing he could do with what they had to work with. Religiously, twice a day, he had taken it upon himself to bathe Allen, change the dressings, apply the soaks. There was no discernible improvement, but he was determined at least to keep the boy comfortable. Week after week it became harder and harder for him to go to Allen's bedside, until finally he had no longer been able to stand the gratitude and dog-like devotion in Allen's eyes. He had turned away, fighting back emotion, found Roche and broken down completely, sobbing.

God save the British. Roche had put him to bed, quieted him and relieved him of any further medical responsibilities. Barks was moved to the far end of the building, and Hooper, the dentist, moved with him. Quiet, wonderful Hoop. Prisoner for over six years. Solid, understanding rock of an Englishman. Hoop, who played the accordion as expertly as Barks had played the violin inexpertly. And it had worked.

As the weeks passed, he had come out of his shell, slowly but surely. And when it had come time for him to be sent back to Sczubin, he was back working in the infirmary. He was sorry that he had to leave. He had even grown fond of Barks.

But why had not the break occurred then? In that moment when it almost did? Why had it waited until later when the end of prison camp was in sight, when he had been vigorous, cheerful, enjoying his work? When he had been admired by all, sought out by all? Why had it happened then, out of the blue, when he had been content, adjusted, eager to return home, his plans thought out, his problems solved?

Back at Sczubin in the fall he had returned from Sagan to find the camp bursting with new prisoners. There were 10 or 12 new doctors, recent captives from the Normandy invasion. Instead of going back into the camp hospital, he moved into one of the barracks with the men. Each barrack now had its own doctor. Much more suddenly than it had come, his depression had gone. All of the enthusiasm and interest had returned. The long, cold, miserable winter, with its snow, its short bleak days, its 17-hour nights, failed to dampen his spirits.

Long cold march, drawing by POW Jim Bickers

The Germans had moved them out, evacuating the camp less than 24 hours before the Russian sweep across Poland had reached them. There was no transportation; they had moved on foot. Long columns of them, flanked by old, miserable, nervous German guards.

He remembered the clear, brilliant days of the march. Ten, twenty degrees below zero. Bright, white, dazzling snow everywhere. The screech of the dry, unpacked snow on the roads as they marched. First south to Znin, then when it seemed that they would meet a Russian salient, the Germans had turned them north and west to Schneidemühl, to Zlotow and finally to Stettin. At nights they slept in barns, farmyards and deserted houses, and by days they marched.

Once they had occupied a deserted village—nothing more than a group of peasant cottages, five or six on each side of a road that stretched into white nothingness in each direction. The German guards had gotten panicky during the night, and when they had awakened in the morning, the one wood-burning truck that had trailed the column and carried old Schneider, the German commander, was gone. The guards were gone. They were free.

Free in the middle of a frozen white nowhere. They spent the day organizing themselves into companies, making plans. They had killed chickens and pigs, roasted them over the fires and gorged themselves until they were sick. Then just at dark the Germans had returned. The men had been restive, unruly, unwilling to give up their freedom, however brief. Some skirmishes had broken out between the men and the guards. But a few bursts from the burp guns, a few dead, a few wounded, and they had become quiet again.

There were enough of them, the prisoners, to have overpowered the small number of Germans who were guarding them. But they were cautious now. All but the impulsive. The end seemed too near. They had survived too long to risk it now. All but the impulsive ones, or the crazed ones. And during the night the occasional pistol shot or the rattle of an automatic weapon took care of them.

Every morning before the march was resumed they had checked the sick and ailing. At every stop they had left a group of men, 20 or 30 or more, in the charge of one of the doctors. The trench foot, the frostbite, the old shrapnel wounds and their general debilitation after long captivity could not tolerate the bitter cold, the prolonged marching.

After eight days only about half of the original column of some 1,200 prisoners was still marching. He and Arthur Mallory, his double-decker bunkmate for the last five months in camp, were still with the marching group. Only he and Colonel Gold had remained of the doctors. Mallory, a Southerner like himself, was a Citadel graduate; had been a company commander in another regiment of his own division; had been captured during the same convulsive battle at Anzio as he. They were inseparable. Every night, whether huddled together in the snow, burrowed into some haystack or sheltered in a barn or farmhouse, they had discussed the merits of leaving the column, joining the sick groups, going it on their own. But by day they were marching again. There was safety in numbers. There was a compulsion, too. Even though their hands were blue and numb, their feet frozen, their limbs exhausted, they were determined to walk as long as there were others walking. There had been his own medical conscience, too, that would not let him abandon Colonel Gold, the other medic and the column. Though he could do nothing, he was conscious that his continued presence (the sorry-assed, lazy pillroller) helped the morale of the others.

He and Mallory had been sorely tempted one night though. At Charlottenburg the Germans had herded them into some outlying farm buildings of a tremendous estate. The manor house, in its setting of snow, an icy wonderland of crystalled trees, its gingerbreaded gables and piazzas shimmering in the cold, blue moonlight, had looked like a picture out of a fairy story. They had lined up for chow, the inevitable thick barley soup that tasted to them like no 10-course meal could ever hope to, and when it had been doled out to them, they had slipped unnoticed into the house itself.

After they had eaten, they had explored some of the ground floor rooms. In the library they had unexpectedly come upon a group of

German officers busy over maps. He had identified himself, and on a pretext of some medical nature, had requested permission to look through the house for some drugs and medicines. Whether it had been his boldness, or the Germans' preoccupation with their own steadily worsening predicament in the face of the Russians, they were allowed to go on.

They had spent the night in one of the upstairs rooms, in the luxurious warmth of the unheated house. There were at least two more levels above them, with enough nooks and crannies, closets and passages to hide 50 men. They had debated long and hard that night whether to stay on, and in the end had fallen asleep undecided. In the morning they had rejoined the others and the column.

When the march had reached Stettin, there were almost 150 more of the men who could no longer go on. He and Colonel Gold had conferred, and Gold had ordered him to remain with this group. The Germans agreed to move these by transportation some way. It had been easy to include Mallory in with the ailing. The rest walked on.

They were taken to the rail yards and loaded into two open coal cars; a tarpaulin sheltered them from the snow. They were several days en route before they reached Berlin. The German rail system was having its own problems. He had marveled at the obstinate tenacity of the methodical German mind that was concerning itself with moving two carloads of ailing POWs while their homeland was disintegrating around them.

Three nights in the rail yards north of Berlin. Three nights back in the almost forgotten sounds of war again. There were day bombings, night bombings. *Amerikanishe Luftgaustern!* But miraculously no hits close to them. Then somehow their two cars had moved on again.

Stalag III-A at Luckenwalde, south of Berlin, was the central camp that the Germans had chosen as a collection point for the prisoners evacuated. The seriously ill in the group that he had cared for were sent to the large prison camp hospital nearby that had serviced the camp, and he and Mallory had gone into a crowded barracks in the officer area. There were men from all nations—Danes, Norwegians, French, British, Greeks, Yugoslavs, New Zealanders, Indians, South

Africans. The prospect of German collapse and the war's end created an atmosphere of excitement, joviality, fellowship. They were all busy, bursting with ideas and plans for the future. Impractical, wonderful dreams of travel, adventure, comradeship. They would never forget one another, forever united in the brotherhood of common deprivation and suffering. It had been a most stimulating and exciting time for him.

When typhus and scarlet fever had broken out in the RAF barracks near theirs, he had volunteered to move in and care for the sick. He had had to climb through a window with his supplies; the Germans had nailed and boarded the entrances and placed it under quarantine. He had been overjoyed when a group of his own enlisted men, the ones who had been captured with him at Anzio, showed up in the enlisted compound. He managed to get Prather, Morrow and Beary into the officers' area and into the barracks with him. They were kept busy for several weeks, nursing and treating the sick. Then he himself had become feverish, ill. It had been more than just exhaustion. High temperatures, chills, cough—he had diagnosed himself as having bronchopneumonia. When it seemed that he was not improving, he had been sent as a patient to the nearby camp hospital.

There had been no beds available in the already overflowing hospital compound, and he was taken over and cared for by a group of the enlisted Irish hospital corpsmen who prepared a bunk for him in their own quarters. They had nursed him carefully, constantly, and within a week he had begun to improve. Capable Sergeant Dennis, in charge of all the enlisted hospital personnel, and Corporal Ryan had made him their charge. Aloysius "Paddy" Ryan—the cheerful Irish gnome, endowed with all the magic of the green island's Little People.

Also in the quarters with him was a young American private, a simple mountain boy from the Kentucky hills. Like himself, a patient, taken over by the corpsmen as one of their own—almost a mascot. The boy, already "round the bend," stared into space, seldom spoke, but responded in automaton fashion to the suggestions of his guardians. Dennis, Ryan and the other corpsmen accepted his condition as one of the inevitable tragedies of war and prison-camp life. They ministered to his every need—fed him, sheltered him, comforted him—with all the care of an elderly mother with a Down syndrome child. The boy was a simple schizophrenic, detached from reality, but there was an occasional spark. Along with Ryan he had become fascinated with the boy and had spent much of his convalescent time trying to break through the barrier, trying to communicate with him. But their efforts had proved futile.

When he had gotten stronger, and when a bed had become available, he moved at Sergeant Dennis' suggestion to a ward in one of the main hospital, barrack-type buildings, which housed the office of the senior medical officer in command of the hospital. Through Dennis he had been introduced and taken into the inner circle, the security group present in every prison compound, which set the policy of internal resistance, received information from outside contacts, assumed responsibility for the welfare of the prisoners. There were no more than five or six men in the group, headed by an elderly, but brilliant and dignified, General Antonich, formerly in command of the Yugoslav military medicine; Millos, a younger Yugoslav; Morin, the French surgeon; Anton, the Pole; and two others—all European—whom he had met only on one occasion, and whose names he had not learned. All were doctors except Sergeant Dennis. He was the only American, and they had made him welcome.

The clandestine meetings, held after the hour of the nightly German-imposed blackout, by the flickering light of a wick in an oleo can, were like episodes from a cloak-and-dagger novel of intrigue. His poor French and his fragmentary knowledge of German and Italian made him ashamed of his own better-than-average American education and increased his admiration and respect for these men, all of whom spoke at least three languages and carried on their discussions in English in deference to him. All had interesting tales to tell of their own experiences; all had been prisoners for over five years; all had maintained their integrity, devotion to medicine and sanity over the years of confinement. None of them shared his naïve enthusiasm for the accomplishments of the Russians. They were more than apprehensive about their future in the hands of their liberators-to-be. They had chided him amusedly on his youthful faith in the goodness of man, his all-American innocence. But of course he had not been convinced. It was the Old World outlook against that of the new, the centuries-old sophistication (that was no longer cynicism) of the continental grandparent against the brash, adolescent grandchild. Mellow vintage wine against raw corn whiskey. The nightly philosophical discussions had helped him mature.

[Ed. Note: the following paragraphs (italicized) are included here, but were stricken by the author:]

He had still been weak, and occasionally mildly feverish, but with Sergeant Dennis, who had access to all areas of the hospital compound, he had visited some of the sick he himself had sent in to the hospital earlier. They had been happy to see him, to hear news of the others. They were all waiting, anticipating the end of the war, like he was, which was now expected daily. All except Johnny Camp.

Maj. J. Camp—veteran of the Africa campaign, casualty at Salerno, captured at Cassino, Congressional Medal of Honor holder, executive officer of the camp at Sczubin, efficient, capable Camp—had marched from Sczubin with Mallory and himself, had stayed with the column at Stettin, had marched the whole way to Luckenwalde. He had collapsed a few days later from undernutrition, exhaustion, and had been sent to the hospital. Now he had seemed almost recovered, with some flesh on his bones and color in his cheeks. He had visited him twice with Sergeant Dennis, then on the day of his third visit, Camp had motioned him closer and had confided to him in whispers that he was in communication with Churchill and that his mission in the hospital was to poison all of the doctors who were all part of the secret group.

Except for the weakness that was inevitable after his long bout of fever, he had felt exceptionally well. He had looked forward to each nightfall, impatiently awaiting the blackout signals and his summons to the evening conclave.

And then it had happened—not until then, when there had been no strain, nothing to provoke it.

They had celebrated the birthday of Anton with a bottle of red wine, a hoarded treasure of General Antonich. Morin had played the violin. It had been a calm, pleasant evening. He had returned to his metal-frame bunk in the quiet sleeping ward and had fallen promptly into an untroubled sleep.

He did not know how long he had slept, but quietly he had awakened. There in a corner of the darkened ward, near the ceiling, in soft illumination, was the *crèche* above the altar from the little mountain chapel in Italy. The chapel above Venafro that Raley had avoided. The chapel on the front line between F Company and G Company in which they had set up the aid station. The chapel with the magenta-tiled roof and white walls, built into the hillside on a ledge that projected over the wooded ravine. It had been their home for eight out of every twelve days during the cold, wet fall and winter. Up the mountain paths, eight days on the line, down the mountain paths, four days of "rest" in the regimental area, knee-deep in mud, with the incessant noise of the incoming and outgoing artillery, then up again to their chapel. The chapel that stood out like a bright flare in a dark, empty sky, in full view of the hidden German positions less than six hundred yards away. The chapel that the Germans would bracket with 88s every time they would try to evacuate any of the wounded by day. It had been almost a game that had gone on for over two months while the lines remained static. One of those crazy inconsistencies of front-line combat. You won't be tagged as long as you stay on base. The chapel had been their base, their haven.

They had used the altar as an operating table for the minor surgery that they could perform. They had made bunks for the wounded by suspending litters between the wooden chapel benches. They had gambled and sworn as combat men do. But they had destroyed nothing of the chapel, just as the Germans had refrained from a direct hit. The goblets, the rings, the jewelry, the trinkets, the beads that adorned the Madonna figure in the crèche—gifts from the simple peasant mountain folk—he had forbidden the men to touch, and they had obeyed.

La Chiesa di Madonna della Fondata, aid station, Hill #1083,
drawing by Tom Graffagnino

And now, high in the corner of the darkened ward, the crèche had shown softly before him. He had sat up unbelievingly in the bunk. There it was, Madonna, rings, trinkets and all. And then slowly it had blurred, and in its place was the olive-drab shirt draped from the hanging shade and obscuring the light from the dim bulb beneath it.

Comprehension had come to him, but deep moving emotion would not go. He had slipped quietly from the bunk and knelt by its side, and his eyes were moist. He did not know how to pray, he could not pray to God because he did not believe. But he prayed, at first silently and then aloud.

"Give me strength to overcome my weaknesses. Give me courage in my humility. Give me tolerance and understanding of my fellows. Let me be worthy."

He remembered thinking that it was a beautiful prayer.

They had found him still kneeling and immobile in the morning. And when they had tried to move him, he had resisted. And when they had persisted, he had fought them and had become frenzied and obscene. He had wanted no one but Anton, and when Anton had come, he had clung to him and sobbed against his chest.

That much he remembered, and it had remained clear to him, but he could not sort out the rest with any accuracy.

It had all been clear and orderly up to that point, but somehow, from then on, time had become jumbled. He had difficulty sorting out events and the sequence of things. In periods like these when he was clear, with his thought processes in high gear, he could almost unravel the tangled string of events, places, people. Almost, but not quite, because there were gaps, usually in transition phases from place to place, where there was no recollection. He was aware of his insanity, but he was aware, too (without being aware) that he was improving. The continuity of his more recent moves was more orderly, and his memory of recent events was better.

He was still occupying the corner of the bare room. Still immobile. Still concentrating on his metabolism and physiology. He was in what the psychiatrists call the fetal position, a withdrawal into the womb, reversion to unborn security. He almost laughed aloud at the idea, remembering the cold, barren cell in the German civilian institution at Brandenburg.

It was Brandenburg, too. And it had been shortly after his break. A blurred interval that contained only flashes of a darkened, shattered room of destruction and physical violence had been succeeded by recollections of a train ride in a third-class carriage. He remembered the lacquered wooden-slatted seating, like the old New Orleans street cars of his youth; the apprehensive German guard who had accompanied him; a walk, and a change of transportation; ornate columns flanked by a cemented balustrade. Somehow he felt that it was the Brandenburg Gate—but whether it was, or whether it was the association of some public monument with his known destination, he could not be certain. He remembered the cobbled streets and the three-story, solid building flush with the sidewalk, the steps to the heavy front door, an entrance foyer with a staircase ascending on the left, with its heavy plaster wall, perforated near the bottom step by a decorative oval aperture, which contained a wrought iron curlicue. He had been led up two or three flights, then through a ward. He remembered how strange it had seemed to him—a ward of inmates. They had all looked thin, small, haggard, vacant, in uniform gray hospital clothing, shaved heads. A vast gray room, high ceilinged, bare wooden flooring, with rows of evenly spaced beds, except that they had not looked like beds, only like rows of bassinets in a nursery. He had been led through the room to the rear, and through another small door to a narrow corridor onto which the door of four strong rooms opened. He had been left in one of these.

How long he stayed he could not remember because again the recollection had faded into a timeless episode. But it had been punctuated with flashes of clarity. It was here he remembered the sores on his body—living in his own filth. Climbing the wall to the barred window and looking out into the night, listening to the sound of the whippoorwill and the cuckoo. That had amused him, because in those brief spells of clarity and insight, he had realized his state. He remembered most of all his nakedness and the constant, penetrating cold. The psychiatrists might attribute meaning to someone's assuming the fetal position. It had amused him then, and it amused him now, even though he knew that there was a modicum of truth in their theorizing, since it satisfied the longing of a disturbed mind, to shrink into inconspicuousness, to withdraw from everything external. But had they never considered cold, constant through and through cold? Had they never considered a fetal position the instinctive mechanism for preserving body warmth? Thighs against chest, skin against skin, head ducked so that the warm expired air would not be wasted, dissipated in the cold room. Back against a wall, a corner preferably, so that only a minimum of one's nakedness was exposed to cold and drafty air. He wondered if the theorists had ever been cold.

***

That was why he had almost laughed, remembering the cold and the first bare cell. His attention became distracted then, by some sound, almost inaudible. And since he had been dwelling on that first period, and again was in a similar barren room, he arose suddenly and left the corner, metabolism, physiology, reflection forgotten momentarily. And crossing to the wall with the window, jumping to grasp the ledge, and scrambling up until his hand could reach the wire grating in the window, pulled himself up in a reenactment of some earlier episode, and looked out into the night. It was still, and the treetops were bathed in moonlight, like the many moonlights through the other small windows in this jumbled up recent past. He knew that he was doing this, and doing it deliberately in imitation of himself on previous occasions.

Old luna, and lunacy. The ancients may have been right. Was there some association, some attraction? The sound was there again, and it was the distant baying of a hound, inaudible except to his own sharpened sense of hearing. And since he had no inhibitions, nothing to repress or stifle the slightest whim, he allowed himself the pleasure of replying to the lonely hound, with an answering eerie howl. He did it two or three times, until he tired of the mimicry, and then dropped quietly back to the floor. He paced the room for a moment then crossed over and sat down again, this time near the door on the opposite wall.

Recent time was what disturbed him; he could not truly remember whether it was weeks, months or years since the onset of his illness. Although now that he was more rational and clear he had reasoned purely from knowing that the present time was late summer, September he thought, that it must be months since he had entered the hospital at Luckenwalde in March.

The German civilian institution at Brandenburg had contained at least three buildings. He remembered being taken finally from his original upper floor confinement and living in an open ward on the second floor. But here again there was no way of gauging what time had elapsed, and there were only fragmentary memories of faces and people. There was Salvador Dali, a thin, gaunt inmate whom he had befriended and named because of the resemblance. It was not his name, of course, but that was the only name he had ever called him. Then suddenly he had found himself in another building, this one built around two sides of a courtyard, really a barnyard, because he had been able to look out of the corridor windows below on six or seven cows that were tethered in stalls there. He could recall only little of this building, a long gloomy dining hall, where they ate on metal dishes at long wooden tables. And finally a third more pleasant building, three stories like the rest.

The progress from one to the next and then to the next must certainly have had to do with abatement of his wilder episodes and improvement of his health because in the last of the buildings he remembered a smaller ward with five or six beds on the second floor. He had met there another American, whom he knew only as Frank, and there were a few others from the war like them. But Frank and the Greek boy, Panayotis Kapsabelis, were the only two he could recall accurately. The rhythm of the name had intrigued him, and even now it was pleasing to repeat it. Pana-YO-tis Kapsa-BEL-is, panaYOtis kapsaBELis, from Zante. Nearly all of the rest of the patients were German. But in that building they had not been confined and could wander from floor to floor, or down and outside into an enclosed yard. The weather had turned warmer, and it had been pleasant in that last building.

He could recall none of the doctors who must have treated him, until then. Although he could not recall the name, he recalled with affection the tall, graying German doctor there in the last building. It was he, a kindly fatherly man who had given him three or four mild electric shock treatments. But there was not much more to remember, except that twice he had sat in the office with the doctor, to the side of a roll-top desk. They had had tea brought to them by the striking 16-year-old Inge with the long, golden hair and classic features, who was the doctor's only child. Inge often sat on the steps to the courtyard with him and talked, and he had told her of America. She had been very kind and assured for one of her age, and she did not seem to mind his occasional strange behavior or wandering conversation.

On the good days, and in the late mornings before the noon meal of soup, he had enjoyed wandering around the walled yard. It had a narrow, cinder path that followed the wall about 10 feet in, and between it and the wall, all the way around had been an old garden, now unkempt, overgrown and forgotten. The path circled, within the square of the rock walls, and came back to the entrance of the building. There were always two willow-twig brooms leaning against the side of the building, and he had loved to sweep with them. They were sturdy, European peasant brooms, and they reminded him of all the witches' brooms he had ever seen. The smell of the willow when he would break one of the twigs brought back to him the birdhouse he had built as a child, that he had covered and trimmed with willow twigs so that it had looked like a log cabin. Except that they were more expertly made, the brooms had reminded him too of the crude twig and sapling brooms of the country Negroes in the South that were used to sweep the bare dirt in front of the shacks.

Every day before noon he would sweep the dirt clean near the path in front of the building, and when the young and lovely Inge would ask him why he did this, he would only smile, knowing that he could not find the words in his limited German to explain about the birdhouse and the willow trees along the path he took to school, or about how it was important to have clean dirt in front of a tumbledown shack with geraniums in rusted lard cans on the porch. Or about Loulie (Mrs. Louise Emerson) who, after her long years as a household maid retired back to her old stone shack at Darrow—near the Houmas House—and sat on her porch with her corncob pipe, a twig broom by her cane rocker.

When he did not sweep the dirt, he had liked to sit in the children's sandbox that was back just off the path toward the rear of the courtyard. Sometimes the girl would walk over to him and watch him as he would make designs in the sand, or just let it run through his fingers, or squeeze it between his bare toes. And there was no way to explain this to her either. But these simple pleasures had satisfied something within him, and in many ways, because even then his adult medical self called it occupational therapy.

***

He could not remember clearly how that phase had ended, but one day he and Frank, the other American, had walked through the unlocked gate in the walled courtyard—or had they climbed the wall?—and had gone. Had they been released by the kindly doctor because he thought they were well? Or had they done this on their own? Or was there something missing that he could not recall?

He remembered paths through woods, cobbled streets and finally a corner somewhere in a town or village, sturdy peasant women in aprons and head bandanas. Groups of young, red-faced Russian soldiers, lounging, joking. The women were working over steaming cauldrons of thick, hot soup. He and Frank had joined a queue, somehow found containers, and had been doled out a wonderful, but strongly flavored stew of meat, potatoes and heavy dumplings. No one seemed to mind their presence.

That same day, too, after the meal, they had gone through a gate in a white picket fence, across a yard of trees to an imposing house to find the Russian officer who was supposed to be in charge of the area. They had gone into his office unannounced and had told him who they were, and had asked how they could find their way to the Americans or to an American hospital. But he had not seemed to understand. And again they had wandered. And later—he did not know when, the same day? the next day?—toward evening the two of them had been walking along, beside and below a railroad track, and, either because they had been directed or because they thought they had found what it was they were looking for, they had crossed the track, climbed a high wire-mesh fence and headed for a large modern-looking white building.

Again the events became tangled. He and Frank had become separated. He remembered a room on the ground floor, unfurnished and cold like the one he was in now, with one door that opened to a corridor and another that opened to the outside. They were never locked, and he came and went as he pleased. It was a hospital of some kind and staffed by the Russians, and from the interior architecture of the building his room was in, it could have been a fairly new German jail of some type—since the rooms in the center of the building opposite his were in cell block arrangements as in a penitentiary. It was very strange, but it did not concern him greatly.

The circumstances surrounding his departure from the Russian-German hospital were not clear. He remembered one day getting into a familiar, boxy, olive-green ambulance with the red cross on its sides, riding alone in the back and occasionally changing seats with the driver's assistant. Frank had reappeared briefly, but his only view of him was through the back window of the ambulance. For some reason Frank was riding in a small European car, along with another person driving and a stocky middle-aged female who sat between them. She looked like Gwelda, who used to play the piano with her girlfriend, Jerry, at the 500 Club Bar on Bourbon Street. The car had followed the ambulance for a while, with Frank waving gaily from the side window, and then was gone forever. He never saw Frank again.

They had made two stops on the trip westward, but he knew not where, although both were in fairly large towns. On the first he had spent a night in a large open ward of an old-fashioned, European hospital that was staffed by Irish nuns. He could remember only some kindly nuns who were dressed in a gray simple habit. He could not remember traveling again, but there was a British hospital later on in a larger city. It had been more modern, and he must have been in a quiet period because he remembered a private room on the second floor, in which he rested in a regular, civilian hospital bed with white sheets and soft blankets. The window had been open, and on the sill was a potted plant that looked like a peony.

And then nothing until he became aware he was in Liège and in an American Army hospital. The section for the disturbed patients had been in a newly constructed, square, one-story wooden building that occupied a corner of a courtyard formed by an L of permanent hospital buildings. The building itself was fenced in by wire from the rest of the open, graveled yard. It had been pleasant there, and it had been good to taste familiar food again—and have it in unlimited amounts. He had become more rational, at least in his own mind and had begun then to pick up the threads and sort some of the fragments. He was still

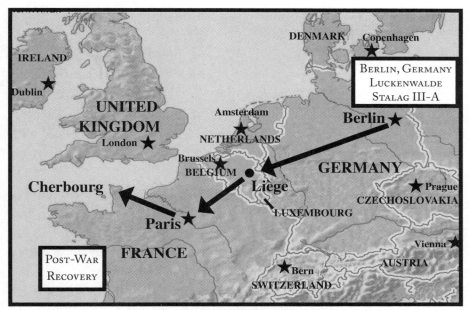

Luckenwalde to Cherbourg
March – July 1945

unaware that he had been listed as missing for almost four months, that his wife and his family had been frantic in their efforts to locate his whereabouts. It was July then.

Once after he had learned that his old division had taken part in the Southern France landings and had been fighting in Alsace, and then in Munich, he had become convinced that they were bivouacked just beyond a hilly knoll that he could see off to the south of where he was. No one had believed him, and so, because of the American Indians that he knew were in his regiment, he had built a small fire in one of the rooms that had an open skylight vent and, with a blanket, was sending smoke signals to his friends. For his efforts he was placed in a canvas straightjacket for several days. He had never seen one before, and it was not uncomfortable. He had thought it a great joke.

He must have been in Liège for several weeks? And then moved again by ambulance to Paris. He had never been to Paris before, and the thought of it excited him. Even from the back of the ambulance it had seemed lovely. He was unfamiliar with the city, but he was able to identify the Seine. He thought he had convinced the ambulance driver to take them all to a sidewalk café for wine near the river bank, but the boy must have been frightened, and instead turned off away from the river, and had unloaded his strange cargo at another American General Hospital. This again was an old-but-pleasant, permanent hospital with trees and lawns and many sprawling buildings that had been taken over by the army medical corps.

He had jumped from the ambulance when it stopped, fully intending to go off on his own back to the Seine, and his anger with the driver had been great. It had been short lived, however, for he had spied a lovely, golden-haired girl in a Red Cross uniform, sitting alone on a grassy lawn, and had run over to sit and talk with her. She was knitting calmly, surrounded by balls of red, yellow, green, blue and pink wool. She did not mind sitting and talking to him, and the brilliant colors of the wool had fascinated him. She had given him one when they had come for him, and he had gone quietly, enjoying the feel of the soft, wool ball. It was a bright red one.

He had seen nothing of Paris except the hospital, but, with his strength and physical condition improving, he had become calmer. He remembered the train station in Paris and the ride by hospital train to Cherbourg. The hospital ship he was on had developed trouble, and at the Canary Islands they were transferred across a gangplank to another ship for the rest of the trip. Sometime during the trip he must have again become agitated, disturbed, because he was confined to a lockup. He had spent his time drawing. He drew fairly well and had covered tablet after tablet with quick sketches of people, events and objects. He still had some of them, old Mihler, the ancient German sergeant from the front lines at Anzio, the brass door-knockers on the front door of the old house in Virginia. the washing troughs from the barracks at Sczubin, with the signs on the walls above:

WASSER SPAREN! RAUCHEN VERBOTEN!

***

Jane and his mother and father had met the ship when it docked at Charleston. He saw them briefly before loading onto the bus that took him to the hospital with the others. He was bursting with things to tell them—his experiences, his plans—and he had talked incessantly, but there had not been much time. Later at the hospital they had visited him, and they had taken him for a ride around the campgrounds, but he had been uneasy. Once he had made them stop, and he and Jane had gotten out and sat on the ground amidst the gnarled roots under one of the larger moss-draped oaks. He had tried to explain to her the attraction of an oak tree, the interesting convolutions of the roots, like those of a Rackham drawing, like those in front of Aunt Mary's house on Amelia Street where he used to play, the dark moist soil with its smell of rotting acorns. He had wanted them to drive off with him and take him home. They had wanted to, but they had not been able because he knew that the car was receiving its control through the radio aerial and that the bastards in the hospital were making it circle back to them. They were crying when they left him at the hospital, and he had been angry.

And now here he was in Texas. Hot, broiling, September Texas. The doctors were doing their best, but there was still a lot for them to learn about mental illness. Except for one or two of them, he did not think they knew much about their business.

LEOMINSTER (MA) - JULY 9 (1945)

GRAFFAGNINO IS LOCATED IN BELGIUM

Medical Corps Captain, Prisoner of War, Husband of Leominister Woman, in Hospital ----------

Mrs. Jane (Drury) Graffagnino, 790 Main street, received word from the War Department over the weekend that her husband, Capt. Peter C. Graffagnino, Medical Corps, U.S. Army, has been located in Liège, Belgium, where he is a patient in a hospital there.

Capt. Graffagnino, who holds the Silver Star Award, the Presidential Unit Citation, and the Medical Badge, was taken prisoner by the Germans at Anzio on February 23, 1944. He has been overseas since June, 1943.

When the Germans capitulated, no word was heard from the medical corps officer and following several weeks of searching by the War Department, Mrs. Graffagnino has received definite word that he has been located and is now safe. The War Department message said he would probably return to the States soon.

P.C. Graffagnino, In U.S. Hospital

LEOMINSTER, July 9–Capt. Peter C. Graffagnino has been located in an American hospital at Leige. by his wife, Jane (Drury) Graffagnino of 790 Main street, from the War Department. Capt. Graffagnino, who holds the Silver Star medal, went overseas in June, 1943, and was taken prisoner by the Germans Feb. 23, 1944.

No word from him had been received since V–E Day. The message said he was he was a patient in the hospital but probably would be home soon.

Reproduced to simulate original clippings.

Part Five

Reflections and Afterthoughts

Introduction

The final chapters of the story, previously published editorials that could be described as "Afterthoughts," include Dr. Graff's efforts in later life to revisit some of the places that had by that time become just memories, and to revalidate to his satisfaction first hand that the experiences had been real and not imagined or distorted over time.

Return to Rome
Originally published August 1975

According to most experienced foreign travelers, one should avoid a mid-summer visit to Italy (to Rome, especially) like the plague. This year, in particular, a trip to the Holy City should have been more of a trial since, in addition to the usual crush of tourists, some two million pilgrims from all over the world were expected for the regular, quarter-century Holy Year celebration.

In spite of such warnings, Luther Wolff, Mary Will Wolff and I have just returned from Rome where we attended the 31st anniversary, Fifth Army Reunion and a medical meeting of the Excelsior Surgical Society. Rome is always crowded, and adding even the pilgrims and the Fifth Army returnees to its usual bustle and confusion didn't seem to make that much difference. Unbelievably, the weather, instead of being hot and suffocating, was pleasantly cool, clear and spring-like for the whole week we spent there.

General Mark Clark, who led the triumphant Fifth Army into Rome in June 1944, was, again, the featured attraction this year. Now, at almost 80 years, he is still the straight, tall, imposing figure, still the ultimate diplomat and still capable of delivering in a forceful voice an inspiring address, modulated with just the right touch of humility and humor. A remarkable man.

We did not always feel so charitably toward the general. To many of us who had come up through North Africa and then served under Patton with the Seventh Army in Sicily, our experiences with Clark's Fifth Army in Italy left something to be desired. In later years, however, we've come to realize that the Seventh Army's problems were almost nonexistent as compared to those of the Fifth. In Sicily the campaign was short, the weather dry, and we were chasing Germans whose only objective was to get out swiftly by deliberate plan—an objective they accomplished quite efficiently according to their own well-worked-out schedule. Patton and the Seventh Army undoubtedly took too much credit for the quick Sicilian victory. In contrast, the Fifth Army faced Germans who were determined to resist, and who retreated only to reach their well-prepared line of defense. In addition, the Allied troops had to endure the miserable weather of two falls and winters, flooded rivers, knee-deep mud and impassable mountain ranges without the benefit of modern helicopter service. The Fifth Army Command also had to contend with the problems of coordinating the movements and pacifying the conflicting interests of such disparate troops as the British, Australians, Indians, Canadians, New Zealanders, South Africans, Free French, Moroccans, Algerians, Turks, Greeks, Italians, Italian Partisans, Brazilians and Poles. It also suffered the chronic lack of support of a secondary front constantly competing for men and material with the build-up for the invasion of Normandy, which came off just one day after the delayed capture of Rome. But to the lowly infantryman who had breezed jauntily through North Africa and Sicily, the discomforts, confusions, seeming chaos and turtle-like progress up the Italian peninsula was a frustrating and inexplicable change. Unfortunately, General Clark (admittedly more of a diplomat and public-relations expert than a specialist in military strategy and tactics) often got blamed for whatever went wrong.

Anyway, this visit to Rome, under the umbrella of General Clark and his Fifth Army command group, was an experience that no ordinary tourist could ever hope to duplicate on his own. This was a five-day gala that included a spectacular welcoming cocktail party at the Villa Maiani on a hill west of the city, with all of Rome, bathed in golden evening sunshine, spread out beneath it; an outdoor special audience with the Pope in St. Peter's Square (the first descent of a Pope from his balcony onto the square itself in 35 years); a reception at the Barberini Palace given by the Italian Minister of Defense; a colorful and emotional memorial service on July 4 in the American military cemetery at Anzio-Nettuno, followed by a two-hour luncheon at an outdoor terrace restaurant overlooking the sea, and followed, still later, by a diplomatic reception and party at the Villa Pariola as guests of U.S. Ambassador Volpe and his wife. A final cocktail party and banquet the next day reassembled all of the guests and dignitaries on the Via Vittorio Veneto at the Excelsior Hotel which had served as General Clark's temporary headquarters 31 years ago in Rome.

Medically, we were also well entertained. The small group of Excelsior Surgical Society members, all of whom had been in Italy during the war as part of the 2nd Auxiliary Surgical Unit attached to the Fifth Army, were guests of the Surgical Staff at Rome's Polyclinic in the University Medical School. Dr. Pietro Valdoni, the retired chief (whose name commands the same respect as that of a William Mayo), and Dr. Paolo Biocca, the present surgical division head, presented an excellent scientific program one day and gave us a comprehensive tour of the facilities there on another day.

In the second week, the various individuals and groups that made up the 160 or so Fifth Army returnees, scattered throughout Italy, Europe and the Mediterranean area in pursuit of their own interests. Our small Columbus contingent, along with Dr. and Mrs. Charles Rife from Milwaukee, rented a car and toured, revisiting old spots remembered from the war years, and eventually headed north through Italy into Southern Switzerland.

One medical highlight of our personal excursion was a visit in Pavia with Dr. and Mrs. Aldo Moschi (who had spent last year here in Columbus, learning the secrets of athletic knees from *Professore* Jack Hughston) and an extensive tour of the University of Pavia Medical School. Another was a visit to the luxurious Villa d'Este at Cernobbio on Lake Como, where Wolff, returning to the elegant quarters he once ruled over as sole American Commandante of the former Luftwaffe hospital, swapped stories with the concierge, who had also been there during the war years.

Except for a flat tire on the way back to Rome and the airport, the whole trip went off without a hitch. And if anyone tells us again that a visit to Italy in the summertime is not worth the trouble, there are three of us, at least, who will certainly disagree.

Goodbye to the C-Ration
Originally published March 1979

ABOUT TWO MONTHS ago the Army announced that the old C-ration was to be no more; it would be phased out over the next three years. An Atlanta paper, commenting on the announcement, editorialized that no GI would ever mourn the passing of either the C- or K-ration. It was clear, however, that the anonymous editorialist had never been intimately acquainted with either of the original field rations. In regard to the C-ration, he wrote that "they tended to such delicacies as powdered eggs, powdered milk and inedible sausage and ham," and of the K-ration, that its main course was a small can of Spam, "a dish that will live in infamy." He viewed both with terror and as "food unfit for human consumption."

Well, while no gourmand ever went into ecstasy over either the K- or C-ration, the editorial judgment was much too harsh. As a former consumer of both during World War II, we feel an obligation to rise in defense and set the matter straight.

In the first place, the C-ration, as most of us knew it in 1942, was a two-can meal; a heavy, main course can, and a lighter, second can of dry biscuits, powdered coffee or cocoa and a few hard candies. There were only three variations of the main course: meat and beans, meat and potato hash, meat and vegetable stew. We found the C-ration a great improvement over the earlier, standard field ration, which usually consisted of a waxed-paper-wrapped sandwich of dry bread and a slice of salami, thrown at you by the mess sergeant as you filed by. The main trouble with the C-ration in combat, when you often had to eat it for days on end, was its weight and bulkiness. Besides being uncomfortable to carry, it was almost impossible to stuff a two-day supply of cans into an already crowded backpack.

The K-rations, which appeared about the same time in 1942, were more suited to the demands of combat since they were one-unit meals neatly packaged into a double cardboard carton about the size of a Cracker Jack box. The outer cardboard layer was heavily waxed and waterproofed and could serve as a container for liquid if necessary, or burned to heat whatever needed to be heated. They were light, compact, and a day's ration of three boxes could easily be packed or stashed away into some pocket. If we remember correctly, the early K-rations came in two varieties: a breakfast ration, with a small, flat can of congealed powdered eggs with ham bits; and a dinner ration, with a similar can of deviled ham or chicken pâté. In addition, each package contained three oblong, hardtack biscuits, a small D-bar of rock-like chocolate, powdered coffee or lemon drink or bouillon, some sugar and a flat package of four cigarettes (usually Wings, Avalons or Twenty Grands).

No such ingredients as powdered milk, sausage, ham or Spam ever appear in the C- and K-rations we consumed in 1942 and 1943. And as for Spam being unfit to eat, we disagree. Actually, we remember it with much affection; a slightly warmed, 1/4-inch slab of Spam was the delectable treat we looked forward to once a week during our prison camp days (two slices on Thanksgiving and Christmas). Compared with the worm-eaten potatoes and a watery stew of horsemeat scraps, tough cabbage leaves and rotting kohlrabi, Spam was delicious . . . but it came out of Red Cross parcels, not C- and K-rations.

There were times in combat when, for two or three weeks in a row, we ate nothing but C- or K-rations. All soldiers were gripers and combat infantrymen were no exception; of course we griped about the monotony of C- and K-rations, but even the dullest GI came up with ways to break the monotony. You liberated a small, carrying-size pot or pan from some peasant house, kept an onion or two always in your pack, scrounged whatever else you could find in the gardens or fields— peppers, fennel, tomatoes, horse beans, garlic, a real egg occasionally— and with a little heat, ingenuity, and a main course can, could concoct a very appetizing meal.

Not all GIs will be glad to see the old C-ration disappear; some of us who remember it fondly will hate to say goodbye. The only real gripers about Army field rations were the "rear area bastards," conditioned to comfort and luxury foods, who were served them occasionally on plates in a permanent mess by some uninspired mess sergeant. C- and K-rations were the combat soldier's best friends. In a combat area, where most of the civilian population was starved for food, if you could no longer stomach them yourself, you could always trade them for anything—even wine and women.

Memories of the Holocaust
Originally published June 1978

Last month, NBC's televised four-part program, "Holocaust," occasioned much comment and stirred up many memories. It was a bit unsettling to some of us, who had experienced, at first and second hand, some of the hardships of those disruptive war years in Europe, to hear comments about exaggeration, media propaganda and even disbelief about some of the events pictured.

On April 30, 1945, our old regiment, the 45th Division's 157th Infantry, captured the city of Munich and set up its command headquarters in the famous Hofbrauhaus, site of the "Beer Hall Putsch" where Hitler made his first bid for power in 1923. Only one day before, on the outskirts of Munich, the Regiment had liberated eight thousand civilian prisoners from a concentration camp at Moosach, and then moved on to the notorious camp at Dachau. The Regiment was under orders to disturb nothing in the camp so that the "international commissions" could investigate conditions there.

Although Heinrich Himmler and the German high command had ordered that all evidence of the Dachau activities be destroyed before abandoning the camp, the speed of the American advance was such that the SS camp officials had fled without completing their work. There were 32,000 starving internees in Dachau on the day of liberation; they represented 41 different national origins, including 1,200 Germans, 600 Dutch, 1,000 Belgians, 700 Hungarians, 300 Austrians, 200 Spanish, 200 Greeks, 4,000 French, 2,000 Italians, 3,000 Slovenes, 1,600 Czechs, 9,000 Poles, 4,000 Russians and 2,500 Jews. In addition, on the rail tracks leading into the camp were 40 open boxcars filled with dead bodies, abandoned by the camp keepers before they could be gotten to the crematoria or into the lime pits for burial. The fields alongside the tracks were also littered with dead, where some of the starved, using their last bit of strength, had climbed out of the cars, tottered a few steps and collapsed. The scenes within the camp—the fetid, overcrowded barracks, the hospital where "patients" had been undergoing "experiments," the gas chambers, the anterooms of the furnace ovens where emaciated bodies were piled like stacked lumber to heights of eight to ten feet—were even more horrifying.

Many of the records kept at Dachau had been destroyed in the weeks before the camp was liberated, but enough of the meticulous card-index system remained to give an indication of the extent of the operation. In the last four months (January to April, 1945), 14,700 "natural" deaths had been recorded. In five months between June and November 1944, 30,000 Jews had been brought in from other concentration camps for execution and disposal. In three months, January to March 1945, 5,000 "non-aliens" (Germans from foreign countries) had been executed. The sights and smells of Dachau were something that men of the 157th would never forget.

During the winter of 1945, while the 157th was fighting its way through Alsace, Worms, Darmstadt, Aschaffenberg and Nuremberg to Munich, we had been moved out of the prison camp at Sczubin in Northern Poland on the long, forced, winter march to Stettin that eventually ended in Luckenwalde, south of Berlin. At the time the Regiment was liberating Dachau, we had been hospitalized, first in a prison camp hospital near Luckenwalde, then in a German civilian hospital in Brandenburg, which, at war's end, was in the Russian zone of occupation.

From the time of our capture on the Anzio beachhead in February 1944, we had experienced many long days of boxcar travel; up through Italy and the Brenner Pass to a camp north of Munich at Moosburg; then again by boxcar, through Pilsen, Breslau and Posen to Bromberg (Bydgoszcz); later to Sagan in Silesia and back; and finally by open coal car from Stettin to Berlin and Luckenwalde. On many occasions, in the rail yards or on sidings, we saw similar train loads of human cattle, most packed far more densely than our own cars, some headed in our direction, some in the opposite. We were aware that there were concentration camps for civilian internees, and, even before capture, we had freed one such camp during the combat in Southern Italy. We knew a little of the conditions in such camps, and we had heard stories about some of the atrocities, but, as prisoners, we were much too preoccupied with our own miseries to think long about them. It was only on the march out of our camp in Poland that we became conscious of the chaos and complete disruption of a starved population wandering aimlessly, like us, in sub-zero weather along the snow-covered roads, some fleeing the Russians, some the Germans. A few of our fellow prisoners, left in the camp at Sczubin, were freed by the Russians and trekked eastward into the rubble of Warsaw; some saw another notorious extermination camp, Treblinka, on the outskirts there, where the scenes at Dachau had been duplicated. It was the same elsewhere—Buchenwald, Theresienstadt, Belsen, Mauthausen and Auschwitz. A civilization gone berserk.

Many of the men of the 157th Infantry whom we had first met in the spring of 1942, trained with in 1943 and fought with through

Anzio and the Italian campaign in 1944, went on with the Regiment into Southern France and through Germany to the bitter end; many died along the way. Most of us who survived those years are now grandparents, and our memories of the war are still vivid. The NBC program, "Holocaust," may have seemed overly brutal and exaggerated to generations that have followed, but it should serve as a grisly reminder that it could (and possibly will) all happen again.

Holocaust, Follow Up
Originally published August 1978

O VER THE JULY 4th weekend, a few weeks after the *Bulletin*'s article on the Holocaust appeared, we joined a group of 157th Infantry officers at a small reunion in Tennessee and heard more first-hand stories about Dachau. Since then, also, there have been phone calls and letters relating to the subject. All have added to our information and understanding of those terrible times.

There were 18 others at the mini-reunion, all of whom had survived the entire campaign (Africa, Sicily, Italy, France, Germany) with the Regiment, and all had been present at the liberation of Dachau. The common recollection, apart from remembering the appalling human wreckage there, was the unbearable stench of the camp and its surrounding area.

After the invasion of Southern France, several of the men had acquired cameras; one had liberated a 16mm German movie camera and film. We saw, in uncensored detail, slides and movies taken on the spot at that notorious camp on the first day of liberation. The pictures were not very pleasant.

One friend, a battalion commander at the time, calloused and embittered by almost two years of front-line combat and the terrible losses incurred by men under his command (especially at Anzio and Nuremberg), allowed his troops to deliberately execute about 33 German SS guards who had been unable to escape the camp. He was later court-martialled for his responsibility in this incident. Yet he remained, even after the passage of 33 years, unrepentant.

The calls and letters from some of our local physicians have also been instructive. One wrote:

> For us Jews this event remains a permanent painful scar, a living memory. Christians have not always fully grasped the significance of the Holocaust, and Jews have been preoccupied with Jewish loss and pain.
>
> The Holocaust was probably, from root causes and moral lapse, more of a Christian than a Jewish problem. Occurring in a Christian society more than a thousand years old, it is time that Christians also study how this most obscene genocide in history could have occurred. It was not really a part of the war, but started eight years earlier in progressive steps. It was watched by the rest of the Western world in a detached manner that allowed the Nazis to know that they could proceed without any limit. The war merely allowed a more impenetrable screen for the Nazis to work behind.
>
> Jews have failed to grasp that the Holocaust destroyed as many non-Jews as Jews, and in mourning the loss of 6,000,000 Jews we have overlooked the millions of others who died. In our preoccupation with the Jewish loss, we have failed to emphasize the universal aspects of the Holocaust.

Since World War II, major and minor holocausts have occurred, and continue to occur—in Russia's Gulag system, in China, and now throughout Africa and in Cambodia. Humanity and inhumanity, it seems, proceed side by side. We wonder if it will ever change.

Poland Revisited
Originally edited July 1971

"WHAT I LIKE about Americans is that they are always so relaxed." Tadeusz Dominik, a thin, wiry man of about 40, dressed in sandals, dark pants and a sleazy, open-necked purple shirt waved a hand to include all his countrymen and added, "The Polish people are always worried and so tense." If he had been more familiar with current slang, he would probably have said "uptight."

The Poles have every reason to be uptight. For hundreds of years they've led a precarious existence as a nation of conglomerate peoples caught between Russia and Central Europe. They have been buffeted, battered, occupied, reoccupied, divided, subdivided, liquidated, deported and resettled in almost every European war since the 10th century. At the end of World War II, when the Western Allies failed to support their independence, they disappeared behind the Iron Curtain where they continue to exist in uneasy equilibrium under Russian domination. They have no reason to be grateful or trusting of the West; they are even more distrustful of the Russian overseers who have "liberated" them before. The future offers little promise.

Four of us, tourists all, were sitting around one of the low tables in the no-longer-elegant lobby of the Hotel Europejski, drinking bottled plum juice and brown beer. While waiting for the bus to take us to the Warsaw airport and the plane for Vienna, we had been trying to communicate (unsuccessfully) with a young Polish student until his professor, Mr. Dominik, arrived. In fact, during the five days we'd spent in Poland, the opportunities to talk directly with any Polish citizens had been limited.

However, Professor Dominik (he apologized for his unPolish surname, theorizing that some time in the past his ancestors must have come from Southern Europe) was eager to talk. He was head of painting in the School of Fine Arts at Warsaw University and ten years ago had spent six months touring the United States on a Ford Foundation scholarship. In the next half hour he answered all questions freely— about the school system, about medical care, about housing, about his own Communism and new opportunities in the "People's Republic." He insisted that on our next visit to Warsaw he would personally be our guide and show us the real Poland.

Our stay in Poland had been most interesting. Thirty of us, all former prisoners of war (along with 21 wives), had returned to see the prison camp at Sczubin which we left in late January 1945 when the Russians overran it. The group tour had been well planned and organized by the Scandinavian Airlines System in conjunction with Wanda Rudzinski, representing a Long Island travel agency, and the super-efficient Orbis Agency (Poland's equivalent of Russia's Intourist, which runs the major hotels, the buses, car rentals, guide service, tours and tourist shops).

We had arrived in Warsaw on a Saturday afternoon, spent the night at the Europejski and traveled by bus the next morning westward for 150 miles through the Polish countryside to the Hotel Mercury in Poznan, stopping on the way at Zelazowa Wola to visit Chopin's birthplace. We went by bus again the next day for 50 miles to Sczubin where we spent two hours at the old camp, Oflag 64, before going on to nearby Bydgoszcz for an official luncheon and speech making. We returned to Warsaw that evening over another route paralleling the Vistula to spend two more days there at the Europejski.

Of course, just the visit to the old camp itself in company with others who had shared past experiences was worth the trip. Most of the buildings were still there—and in much better shape than when we had occupied them, for the camp is still in use as a reform school for problem boys. Only some of the old wooden barracks, the double fences of barbed wire, the sentry boxes and searchlights were gone. The sole familiar face belonged to the ancient Pole janitor who, in our day, drove the horse-drawn "honey wagon" which pumped out the 12-holer open air latrine and then spread the night soil on the fields across the road.

Nearly all of the countryside through which we traveled going from Warsaw to Poznan, Bydgoszcz and back (in fact, most of Northern Poland from East Germany on the west to Russia on the east) is a vast, flat, fertile farmland. We were told that 85% of the farms are privately owned—at least they are government allotted but privately run with the produce sold on the open market. But the acreage size of the "private" farm is only 15 acres and no more than six in a family may live on it. The acreage of the 15% of collective farms was not disclosed, but the ones we passed were extensive operations and only on these is any mechanized equipment in evidence.

Each farm has its small cottage, its chickens and pigs, its potato mounds, its small orchard and its planted main crop or crops. (The raspberry farms are said to be most profitable.) They are farmed by hand and horsepower and each seemed to have a standard, all purpose rubber-tired wooden farm wagon pulled by one or two horses. There is little commercial fertilizer industry in Poland, and nearly all of the neatly plowed and planted fields were dotted with lines of manure piles, and, in the evenings, solid farm women wielding pitchforks methodically spread them out. Each year most of the trees along the farm borders are trimmed severely back to the trunk, and their stubby, thicket-crowns of new growth are favorite nesting sites for Poland's many old-world storks. There is no wasted or unused land and, in this section, practically no forestland except for small patches of neatly planted government forests. There are no superhighways, and no need for them as the traffic load is minimal; but the two-lane main roads are quite good, well kept and free of litter.

There are no visible gas stations, only an occasional roadside pump in the larger villages or along the streets of the large cities, and nothing comparable to our own service station extravaganzas. At the infrequent rest stops along the roads there is sometimes a small government-run concession stand where you may buy a pallid, weakly carbonated orange drink and stale cookies. Plumbing facilities are rarely present except for the woods, which serve both sexes (ladies to the left, men to the right—and step carefully).

Twenty-six years ago Warsaw was reduced to rubble. In 1944, on order from Hitler, the Germans had methodically destroyed 85% of the city by shelling, dynamiting and fire. As the Russian army approached, its generals had called for assistance and urged the Poles to rise and resist, but for the next 63 days, the Russians waited patiently on the other side of the Vistula and did not move in to "liberate" the city until they were sure the Germans had done a thorough job. Still today, Warsaw is very impressive. At least half of the city and almost all of what is called the "Old Town" has been restored from pictures and old plans exactly as it was in the past. The rest, too, has all been rebuilt, but with wide streets, parks and many large open plazas and squares.

On the outskirts and on a number of city buildings whose outer walls survived, sprays of rifle and machine gun bullet marks can still be seen. New housing projects are scattered throughout with shining, modern, high rise apartments; the open areas between buildings are paved with walnut-sized pieces of rubble painstakingly hand-laid in intricate design. The old, 100-block, walled Ghetto, into which the Germans had crowded 500,000 Polish Jews, is one of these pleasant open projects now, and there is a hauntingly sculptured bronze monument commemorating the heroic leaders of the Jewish Resistance; there is a smaller even more impressive sculpture covering the sewer through which supplies and guns had been smuggled into the Ghetto and eventually, through which a handful of survivors escaped.

Warsaw is a compact, clean and orderly city, and now its population is back to more than a million. There are flowerbeds everywhere, and when we saw them in May, they were filled with pansies in full bloom. Eighty-five percent (the standard statistical figure, it seemed) of its businesses, even the small shops, are government controlled. There is one large modern shopping mall and center in midtown opposite the tall, monstrously ugly, Russian-built Palace of Culture and Science, where there is a large amount of merchandise, expensively priced and poorly displayed.

Housing is still in short supply, and apartments are assigned according to family size; a six-room apartment is a tremendous one. A young couple getting married is allotted two rooms, but must sign and go on a waiting list for three years. There is no pollution and no traffic problem in Warsaw. Automobiles are scarce enough that people gather in knots about any unusual car like the one from Switzerland parked by our hotel. There are no German- or Western-made cars to be seen; the most common car now is the Polish-made Fiat. (The Poles call one Russian-made car, the "Philosopher's Car"—if you buy one you think you own an automobile.) It is everyone's ambition to own a car, but only bureaucrats and officials can afford one. The Warsaw streets are safe and there is no rowdiness; there are no "hippies." The women are liberated, equal and plainly dressed; they work as doctors, officials and guides; they drive cabs, push wheelbarrows, lay sod, sweep streets, dig with shovels and mix cement. Everyone seems industrious and busy—but, like Professor Dominik said, tense. There is not much joviality or open friendliness. Generally, the Poles avoid tourists and strangers and, it seemed, even each other.

Still, when you remember Polish history, that its boundaries have been constantly changing for 10 centuries, that some 250,000 Poles who fought with the West were never able to return home after World War II, that a million or so were eliminated by the Germans, another million by Russians, that an additional three and a half million Polish Jews (who once made up 11% of Poland's population) have all but disappeared, and that a large number of its present inhabitants have been moved about and resettled by decree of the Russian-dominated "People's Republic," you begin to understand why the children look serious and why the adults are wary of strangers.

An old aunt of one of our group (still living as a pensioner in Warsaw) said, "Yes, things are much better now. We live in a nice large concentration camp instead of a small one."

Poor Medics—Gen. Patton Footnote
Originally published September 1963

As an aside to the Patton stories above [in Part One], we doubt that the general had any true and lasting affection for the Medical Corps. This was not unusual among the regular line officers, and in Patton, impatient and dedicated to action as he was, the attitude was even more understandable.

The medics were the stepchildren of the ground forces. They were seldom briefed on operational plans, and on moving into some bivouac area were accustomed to hearing the executive officer groan, "My God, we forgot the medics." Whereupon they would automatically bed down for the night in the only unassigned swamp available. To the line officers we were a necessary but bothersome encumberment in peacetime training and field maneuvers, performing inconsequential and often annoying duties on generally healthy young males. In wartime the medics were belatedly glamorized by the press correspondents and did enjoy at times great affection and respect, particularly among the actual combat troops. It was, however, an affection that diminished in inverse proportion as the distance from front line to rear increased.

Even though General Patton was a front-line soldier and quite attached to his own personal surgeon (Charlie Odom, from New Orleans) who accompanied him throughout the African, Sicilian and European campaigns, the attitude of a lifetime was hard to overcome when it came to praise for his medical troops. After the Sicilian campaign, our regiment, along with all the units of his Seventh Army, was read the following congratulatory general order, excerpted here:

Soldiers of the Seventh Army:
    Born at sea, baptized in blood, and crowned with victory . . . you have added a glorious chapter to the history of war.

Every man in the Army deserves equal credit. The enduring valor of the Infantry and the impetuous ferocity of the tanks were matched by the tireless clamor of our destroying guns.

The Engineers performed prodigies in the construction of impossible roads over impassable country. The Services of Maintenance and Supply performed a miracle. The Signal Corps laid over 10,000 miles of wire, and the Medical Department evacuated and cared for our sick and wounded.

The Infantry was enduring and valorous, the tanks were impetuously ferocious, the Artillery was tirelessly destroying, the Engineers were impossibly prodigious, Supply was miraculous, the Signal Corps outdid itself, and the Medical Department also ran.

Poor medics.

Exercise in Nostalgia
Originally published May 1971

As you read this we could be standing in the brick and cobblestone platz between the two main buildings of the old boys' school in Sczubin. The chances are it will look much the same as it did when we first saw it in May 1944. Beyond the Oder, villages in Eastern Europe and Poland do not change much with the passage of years.

In 1944, Sczubin was the site of Oflag (Offizierlager) 64, the German prison camp for captured ground-force American officers below the rank of full colonel. But it had a longer history. When war in Europe became certain, the Poles themselves had closed the school, built some barracks on its 10-acre grounds and converted it into a billeting area for Polish cavalry. After the blitzkrieg in 1939, the Germans ringed it with barbed wire, added more barracks and turned it into a POW camp. They even renamed the village, Altburgund. Before June 1943, when it became a camp for Americans, the French, British and Russians knew it as prisoners also.

Since the war, a small nucleus of former prisoners has kept an alumni-like organization in existence. On infrequent occasions there have been reunions. (We attended one in New York in 1950—a rollicking, drunken bash at Toots Shor's with entertainment supplied by a talented group of ex-prisoners who, during camp days, had improvised a stage and theater in one of the barracks and helped to relieve our boredom with plays and variety shows.) About four years ago at another reunion in Chicago, the idea of a travel junket to revisit Sczubin was conceived. Finally, this year, after a couple of abortive attempts to arrange one, the tour will take place.

At peak occupancy, there were some two thousand American prisoners in the Sczubin camp. From the list sent out of those planning to make the present tour (about 30, not including wives), only six or seven names are familiar to us. The returnees will be a mixed group; they will range in age from 45 to 70. Nearly everyone will have a different story to tell about how the war ended for him as an individual, for some were left in the camp and were there when the Russians overran it, others dropped by the wayside at different places in Poland and Northern Germany on the eight-week long march to Berlin and Luckenwalde. Nearly everyone, also, will have his own recollections of the camp itself. Some will remember the many tunnel-digging and escape projects, some the amateur theatricals, some the volleyball and softball games. All will remember the endless hours of daylight during the short summer season, the endless hours of darkness during the long winters, and the interminable, grinding days of dull, chronic hunger when food was our chief preoccupation.

It should be an interesting exercise in nostalgia. Not one of us, who remained in or left the camp in the snow and sub-zero weather late in January 1945, would have entertained the thought of ever wanting to see it again. It was not the kind of garden spot where you'd willingly choose to spend a vacation.

But time mellows all, and curiosity overcomes even the least sentimental of us. The chance to see for ourselves whether memory is accurate, or whether it all could have been as miserable as it once seemed, has been too good to pass up. So instead of heading west into the sunset for a medical meeting in Hawaii, we're off in the opposite direction to Poland. At least the snow might be melted by now.

Afterword

The Making of *Dr. Graff Remembers*

This book would never have been created were it not for the devoted efforts of Barbara Skinner Walden (Dent). From the publication of its very first issue in 1955 until her retirement in 1994, she was the executive secretary to the editor of *The Bulletin of the Muscogee County Medical Society* in Columbus, Georgia.

When my dad, Peter Carl Graffagnino, began his tenure as volunteer editor of *The Bulletin* in 1962, his very first editorial included "an unbounded admiration for the capabilities of our attractive and durable Executive Secretary, Mrs. Barbara Walden."

Ten years later, Dad, remarking with some amazement at his own perseverance in his role as editor of the publication, expressed his continuing regard for his enduring executive secretary. Of Barbara, widowed and remarried during the intervening ten years, he wrote in an editorial that appeared in the January 1972 issue:

> For seventeen years now, Barbara Dent, in addition to her
> many other demanding tasks and responsibilities, has supplied

energy, enthusiasm and direction to *The Bulletin* and has been the constant and guiding force behind it. She has managed its finances, pursued its advertisers, typed its papers, arranged its format, corrected its spelling, polished its grammar, proof-read its pages, bedeviled printers, prodded contributors and inspired its part-time editors. Without her the publication would not exist.

Another ten years later, commemorating a full twenty years in his role as editor, he wrote his final editorial, which ended:

> Since the beginning . . . *The Bulletin's* greatest strength has been the constancy of its Executive Secretary, Barbara Dent. . . . Editors do wear out occasionally, so, in vacating the chair, . . . we extend best wishes along with the fervent hope that Barbara will continue to nurse her *Bulletin*—and prod its editors—for an indefinite time to come.

Upon his retirement as editor of *The Bulletin*, Dad shut down his medical practice, sold the house on Lookout Drive and moved a few miles up the road to Hamilton, Georgia, where the plan was to spend his retirement years hunting, fishing, writing and enjoying visits with his four grandchildren.

Fate had other ideas, however. Dad died barely two years later in January of 1984 at the early age of 67, his longtime dream of becoming a "real" author by writing and publishing a book—beginning with his experiences as a medic in World War II—sadly unfulfilled.

But Barbara was not done yet. She continued to serve as *The Bulletin's* executive secretary until her own retirement. It was then she began her own quest to make Dad's dream a reality. With hard copies of twenty years of *Bulletin* issues in hand, a scanner and text-conversion software—both primitive by today's standards—she set out to complete Dad's aspirations.

I first heard of her efforts from my mom, whom Barbara had contacted to determine if the family would agree to allow her to follow up on her desire to publish all of Dad's editorials, which numbered well over 300, published in 240 issues of *The Bulletin* during his tenure as its editor. This body of work contained, in addition to his memories of WWII, reflections and musings on life in the Sixties and Seventies—the politics and the social upheaval of the times, the state of the medical profession—all written with a broad range of insight, humor, angst and at times, outrage.

The family whole-heartedly agreed to Barbara's request. I became Barbara's co-conspirator in her efforts and began to build a web site with Dad's writings as the electronic output of her efforts became available. Her work with the scanner was not completed until 2002, when I received a "complete set" of diskettes containing a formidable collection of MS-Doc files. Now it appeared there remained only a few final tasks: to find an interested publisher, to perform the final editing of the text and to organize the material into a readable and presentable format.

Before the project could progress to the next level, however, Fate played another card from the bottom of the deck: Barbara passed away in 2006, and the project went back into semi-hibernation. Now it was her dream, as well as Dad's, that had been frustrated and unfulfilled.

Thanks to Barbara's daughter, Dr. Pamela Walden, the story did not end there. Wanting to see her mother's years of hard work and dedication completed, she contacted the Graffagnino family by e-mail to let us know it was her wish to continue her mother's efforts. She would take on the task of finding a suitable and willing publisher.

Pamela wrote this about her mother's commitment to publishing Dad's journalistic endeavors:

The publication of this book is a tribute to my mother, Barbara, and her dedication to seeing that Dr. Graff's literary efforts, which she so greatly admired, might be read and enjoyed by a greater audience.

My mother always had a very strong work ethic. She had taken her job as Executive Secretary of the Muscogee County Medical Society not long after my birth in 1956. My father died when I was only 8. Several years later, following the sudden death of her second husband, I saw Mother not only sustain a livelihood, but continue to flourish in her work. She was a role model for me.

As I moved from place to place in pursuit of my dance career, she was always supportive. My dissertation would never have been completed without her commitment to transcribing the many hours of tapes I had collected from my case studies. She was dedicated, not only to me, but to her passion for good writing.

Sometime after her retirement in 1994 as Executive Secretary for the Society and the editorial assistant for *The Bulletin*, my mother began this project to see Dr. Graff's works—which had been such a significant focus of her professional career for twenty years from 1962 to 1981—published as a book.

In the early stages of this project, I would call and ask her how she was and what she was doing. Her frequent reply was "I am working on my book." Today, looking back, I wish I had been more involved with her in the process—but it was her own special project. I believe her dedication to the compilation of Dr. Graff's editorials allowed her to continue to exercise her meticulous skills and sustain her sharp mind.

When she passed suddenly in 2006, I did become more involved and knew the most important task for me would be to make sure her project would be completed and her efforts rewarded.

— Leslie Pamela Walden, Ed.D.

Dr. Walden's efforts, after much research and inquiry, resulted in her introducing the project to a dear friend and journalism professor, Dan Cabaniss, whose stepmother, Micki Cabaniss (Eutsler), owned Grateful Steps, a traditional, independent publishing house in Asheville, North Carolina. This was an inspired choice as it turned out, primarily because Micki herself had spent a number of years in Columbus, Georgia, and had been an obstetrical physician colleague of Dad.

I agreed to resume my own participation in the effort and have subsequently spent many hours on the phone with Micki over a period of many months, meticulously reviewing every line of text for spelling, punctuation, clarity and editorial consistency. It has been an enlightening experience for me, in particular, to learn what an editor really does to prepare an author's work for publication.

I am deeply indebted to both Pamela and to Micki for their contributions toward fulfilling the dreams of both my dad and of Pamela's mom by helping make this book a reality.

— R.D.G.

MAPS

All maps are modified from CIA Maps in Public Domain except for Anzio-Nettuno,which is modified from a Google Map in Public Domain.

SELECTED REFERENCES

Bickers, James F., Jr. *Oflag 64, Fiftieth Anniversary Book*. Evanston, IL: Evanston Publishing, Inc. , 1993.

Medical Department, Fort Benning, Georgia. *Historical and Pictorial Review, Medical Department, Fort Benning, Georgia 1942*. Los Angeles, CA: Army and Navy Publishing Company, 1941.

Muscogee County Medical Society. *The Bulletin of the Muscogee County Medical Society*. Columbus, GA: 1962–1980.

The 157th Infantry Regiment. *Eager for Duty*. Baton Rouge, LA: Army & Navy Publishing Company, 1946.

The Forty-Fifth Infantry Division. *The Fighting Forty-Fifth, The Combat Report of an Infantry Division*. Baton Rouge, LA: Army & Navy Publishing Company, 1946.

Vaughan-Thomas, Wynford. *Anzio: the Massacre at the Beachhead*. New York, NY: Holt, Rinehart & Winston, 1962.

Illustrations

Cover Illustrations: Front cover. Dr. Peter Carl Graffagnino. From personal photo collection of Peter Carl Graffagnino. War scenes (clockwise from top): see credits for same photos pages 165, 83, 80 and 65, respectively. Back cover. Peter Carl Graffagnino. From personal photo collection of Peter Carl Graffagnino. Original art (left to right): Col. Ankcorn. Watercolor by Peter Carl Graffagnino. Venafro church. Sketch by Tom Graffagnino. Jack "Blake" Blumberg. Watercolor by Peter Carl Graffagnino.

Page x. Family portrait. From personal photo collection of Peter Carl Graffagnino.

Page 4. Dr. Peter Carl Graffagnino. From personal photo collection of Peter Carl Graffagnino.

Page 9. Fort Benning Medical Office Building. From *Medical Department, Fort Benning. 1941*. Los Angeles, CA: The Army and Navy Publishing Company, Inc. West Coast Office, p. 33. Deemed in public domain.

Page 11. Fort Benning Main Headquarters Building. From *Medical Department, Fort Benning. 1941*. The Army and Navy Publishing Company, Inc. West Coast Office, p. 49. Deemed in public domain.

Page 13. Fort Benning Station Hospital. From *Medical Department, Fort Benning. 1941*. Los Angeles, CA: The Army and Navy Publishing Company, Inc. West Coast Office, p. 33. Deemed in public domain.

Page 15. Max Rulney. From *Medical Department, Fort Benning. 1941*. Los Angeles, CA: The Army and Navy Publishing Company, Inc. West Coast Office, p. 11. Deemed in public domain.

Page 23. Wm. G. Love, Jr. From *Medical Department, Fort Benning. 1941*. Los Angeles, CA: The Army and Navy Publishing Company, Inc. West Coast Office, p. 13. Deemed in public domain.

Page 24. Bell M. Harvard. From *Medical Department, Fort Benning. 1941*. Los Angeles, CA: The Army and Navy Publishing Company, Inc. West Coast Office, p. 12. Deemed in public domain.

Page 25. Lee F. Blackman, Jr. From *Medical Department, Fort Benning. 1941.* Los Angeles, CA: The Army and Navy Publishing Company, Inc. West Coast Office, p. 12. Deemed in public domain.

Page 27. Peter C. Graffagnino. *From Medical Department, Fort Benning. 1941.* Los Angeles, CA: The Army and Navy Publishing Company, Inc. West Coast Office, p. 12. Deemed in public domain.

Page 33. Army training exercise. From personal photo collection of Peter Carl Graffagnino.

Page 34. Major Chet James. From *Eager for Duty.* Baton Rouge, LA: Army & Navy Publishing Company, 1946, p. 6. Deemed in public domain.

Page 43. Dr. P.C. Graffagnino. From personal photo collection of Peter Carl Graffagnino.

Page 45. Colonel "Uncle Charlie" Ankcorn. From *Eager for Duty.* Baton Rouge, LA: Army & Navy Publishing Company, 1946, p. 6. Deemed in public domain.

Page 51. Allied Landing, Sicily. From *The Fighting Forty-Fifth, The Combat Report of an Infantry Division.* Army & Navy Publishing Company, Baton Rouge, LA: 1946, p. 15. Deemed in public domain.

Page 56. Sicilian donkeys. From *Eager for Duty.* Baton Rouge, LA: Army & Navy Publishing Company, 1946, p. 50.

Page 65. Jack "Blake" Blumberg From personal photo collection of Peter Carl Graffagnino.

Page 75. Salerno Allied troop landing. From *The Fighting Forty-Fifth, The Combat Report of an Infantry Division.* Baton Rouge LA: Army & Navy Publishing Company, 1946, p. 15. Deemed in public domain.

Page 80. Allied troops disarm German shell. From *The Fighting Forty-Fifth, The Combat Report of an Infantry Division.* Baton Rouge LA: Army & Navy Publishing Company, 1946, p. 51. Deemed in public domain.

Page 83. *La Chiesa di Madonna della Fondata,* aid station, Hill #1083 From personal photo collection of Peter Carl Graffagnino.

Page 85. Bucky Behers and Dr. Graff. From personal photo collection of Peter Carl Graffagnino.

Page 87. Christmas Day Services, Venafro, Italy *The Fighting Forty-Fifth, The Combat Report of an Infantry Division*. Baton Rouge LA: Army & Navy Publishing Company, 1946, p. 50. Deemed in public domain.

Page 88. Venafro, Italy. From *Eager for Duty*. Baton Rouge, LA: Army & Navy Publishing Company, 1946, p. 47. Deemed in public domain.

Page 90. Volturno valley. From personal photo collection of Peter Carl Graffagnino.

Page 101. Troops digging Allied defenses at Anzio. From *Eager for Duty*. Baton Rouge, LA: Army & Navy Publishing Company, 1946. p. 70. Deemed in public domain.

Page 102. The Caves of Pozzolana. From *The Fighting Forty-Fifth, The Combat Report of an Infantry Division*. Baton Rouge LA: Army & Navy Publishing Company, 1946, p. 77. Deemed in public domain.

Page 129. Oflag Directory. *Oflag 64, Fiftieth Anniversary Book*. Evanston, IL: Evanston Publishing, Inc., 1993. Deemed in public domain.

Page 161. Jane Drury and Peter C. Graffagnino wedding photo. From personal photo collection of Peter Carl Graffagnino.

Page 165. Chaplain Father Barry leads prayer on Anzio. From *Eager for Duty*. Baton Rouge, LA: Army & Navy Publishing Company, 1946, p. 67. Deemed in public domain.

Page 167. Overpass at Aprilia – "The Flyover." From *Eager for Duty*. Baton Rouge, LA: Army & Navy Publishing Company, 1946, p. 65. Deemed in public domain.

Page 168. Pozzolana caves, scene of Battle of the Caves. From personal photo collection of Peter Carl Graffagnino.

Page 170. Oflag 64, Sczubin (Altburgund), Poland. Drawing by POW Jim Bickers. *Oflag 64, Fiftieth Anniversary Book*. Evanston, IL: Evanston Publishing, Inc., 1993, p. 147. Reprinted with permission from the Bickers family.

Page 173. Long cold march. Drawing by POW Jim Bickers. From Oflag 64 website: oflag64.us/Oflag64/The_Long_Cold_March.html. Reprinted with permission from the Bickers family.

Page 181. *La Chiesa di Madonna della Fondata*, aid station, Hill #1083. Drawing by Tom Graffagnino.

Page 230. Peter C. Graffagnino. From personal photo collection of Peter Carl Graffagnino.

Index

About the Author

Peter Carl Graffagnino was born in New Orleans, Louisiana, February 14, 1916, where he attended Tulane University as an undergraduate and medical student. During his residency at Cornell University in New York, he decided to join the Army. He spent the next two years as a 1st Lt. Army medic in training at a series of Army posts, including Fort Benning outside of Columbus, Georgia, and Fort Devens near Boston, Massachusetts.

In the fall of 1942 while at Fort Devens he met and married Jane Drury of Leominster, Massachusetts, only to ship out the following summer from Hampton Roads, VA, aboard the *U.S.S. Thomas Jefferson* to join the Allied war effort in Sicily and Italy.

He returned home during the summer of 1945 after two years overseas, only to be hospitalized, requiring shock treatments to deal with severe trauma suffered during his experiences in the war.

After a complete and remarkable recovery he returned to New Orleans to complete his medical training in Obstetrics and Gynecology. In 1950 he moved with his wife and their two young sons to Columbus, Georgia, where he set up a highly successful medical practice, going on to become a revered member of the local community.

During his years in Columbus, Dr. Graff served as Editor of *The Bulletin of the Muscogee County Medical Society* from 1962 until he retired from his medical practice in 1981. He and Jane then sold their home on Lookout Drive and moved to nearby Hamilton, Georgia, where they built their retirement home.

Before he could fulfill his retirement dream of writing, hunting, fishing and enjoying visits from his growing troop of grandchildren, Dr. Graff died in January of 1984, just shy of his 68th birthday.

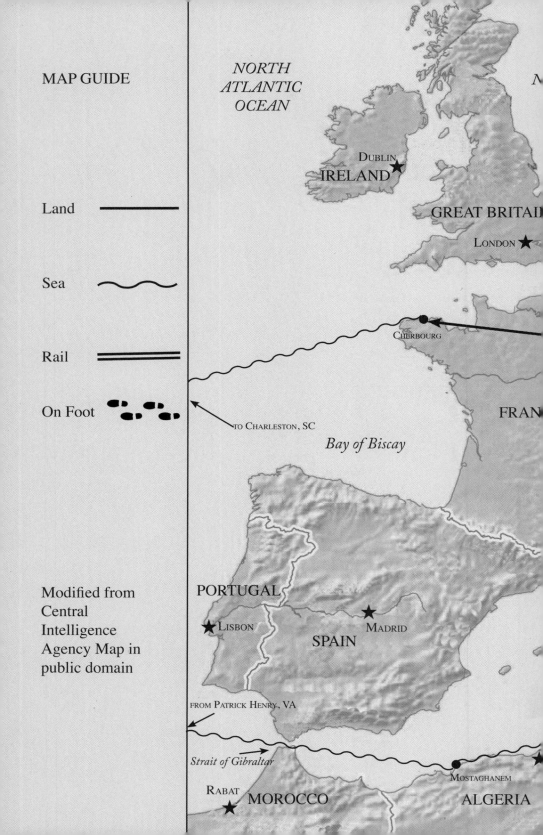